Bleuette
The Doll and Her Wardrobe

This Première Bleuette, also shown on the cover of this book, is costumed in a red cotton faille ensemble made from patterns in La Semaine de Suzette. *White soutache has been added as a contrasting design element. The skirt is attached to a white cotton faille sleeveless top, featuring an embroidered red anchor at the neckline. The jacket closes with two pearl buttons secured by thread loops. Although many different styles of Marine costumes were offered through the catalogs of Gautier-Languereau, this particular costume is made from Pattern #31-33, 1906, "Costume de quartier-maître." (Louise Hedrick's pattern for this costume appears on page 142.)*

Bleuette
The Doll and Her Wardrobe

Barbara Hilliker

Portfolio Press

First edition/First printing

Copyright ©2002 Barbara Hilliker. All rights reserved. No part of the contents of
this book may be reproduced without the written permission of the publisher.

The rights to *La Semaine de Suzette* and all books originally published
by Gautier-Languereau are owned today by Hachette Publishing.

To purchase additional copies of this book, please contact:
Portfolio Press, 130 Wineow Street, Cumberland, MD 21502.
877-737-1200

Library of Congress Control Number 2002107113
ISBN 0-942620-63-1

Project Editor: Krystyna Poray Goddu
Production: Tammy S. Blank

Design by Lynn Amos
Cover design by John Vanden-Heuvel Design
Cover photo by Robert M. Talbot

Printed and bound in Korea

ACKNOWLEDGEMENTS

book is not written in isolation. This book about Bleuette would never have been possible without the help, support and encouragement of others. Their shared knowledge and gift of friendship are deeply appreciated. I especially thank my children and grandchildren for their understanding and encouragement during the years of research and writing. Finally, I want to thank my best friend and husband of forty-six years, Jack, who has offered his love, his wonderful cooking skills, his photographic expertise and his invaluable support to make this book a reality.

My warm thanks go to Becky Moncrief, President of UFDC, who brought Bleuette to the attention of American collectors, and has been steadfast in her support of Bleuette's activities at UFDC. I also thank Bettyanne Twigg, past-President of UFDC, for her encouragement and support.

My gratitude goes to Dr. Hope Werness, professor of art history, California State University, Stanislaus, who helped build the foundation skills in research and writing that have resulted in this book. I also want to thank Krystyna Poray Goddu for her patience and expertise as editor-in-chief of Portfolio Press. She has made the writing of this book a satisfying and positive experience. I appreciate the talent Lynn Amos brought to the design of each page.

I am especially grateful to Louise Hedrick of Elk Grove, Wisconsin, for generously contributing the patterns that make up Chapter 8 of this book. Louise's talent and skill in creating clear concise patterns and instructions for Bleuette's wardrobe are matched only by her enthusiasm for sharing this expertise with other Bleuette lovers.

I would also like to thank the many individuals who shared their dolls, the fruits of their sewing skill and their friendship during the writing of the book. In Paris, my warm gratitude goes to Samy Odin, Director of the Musée de la Poupée, for his unfailing kindnesses in support of my research, and for sharing his knowledge and love for SFBJ dolls and Bleuette with me. Daniel and Hélène Bugat-Pujol offered their gracious hospitality, support and friendship, and shared their expertise throughout the writing. Albert and Claude Bazin shared their home, their talent and their love of doll research. Suzanne Gautrot, who wrote the first definitive book on Bleuette's patterns, shared her knowledge and love of Bleuette, her dolls, her home and her friendship. Barbara Spadaccini-Day and Nicole Offroy-Gandini helped me bridge the English-French gap so graciously, and offered their enthusiastic support for this book. Mathilde Hertier and Nadine Houy shared their great skill as expert seamstresses. Colette Bauer shared her dolls and worked tirelessly to make the photographic sessions move smoothly. Guido Odin generously offered his photographic expertise and advice. Special thanks go to Elizabeth C. Mommee who has searched all over France for magazines, books and documents to further my research.

In the United States, I would like to thank all the subscribers to the *Chères Amies de Bleuette Revue* who have shared their love of Bleuette through photographs and friendship. Special thanks go to Louise Hedrick; Doris Lechler; Deanna Pinizotto; Marcene Oxford; Ruth Brown; Atha Kahler; and Joyce Coughlin, all of whom went far beyond the bounds of friendship in sharing their time, talents and dolls. I thank June and Val Hays for their steadfast support and friendship. I also want to thank Ann Perry for technical graphic and computer support, as well as her friendship, and Debbie Woodall for her styling expertise.

This book would not have been possible without the skilled research of others who have written about Bleuette. My appreciation to Suzanne Gautrot; Hélène Bugat-Pujol; Albert Bazin; Colette Merlen; BillyBoy; Francois Theimer; Anne-Marie and Jacques Porot; Marie-Edith Charles-Mylius; and Gertrude Almquist-Bois.

Finally, all who love Bleuette will forever be in the debt of Gautier-Languereau Publishing (now a part of Hachette Publishing) for introducing Bleuette and her amazing wardrobe through the patterns in *La Semaine de Suzette* and the artful catalogs of her clothing.

Contents

Dolls shown on these pages are described on page 175.

INTRODUCTION

Bleuette: In Old French, the sound of her name is enough to spark the imagination—for a *bluette* is a spark that lights a fire. True to her name, Bleuette set alight the imaginations of young girls for more than half of the twentieth century. Introduced in 1905 as a premium for a new magazine for girls, she is the only doll with a written history covering more than fifty years. From 1905-1960 (with a brief hiatus during the German occupation of France in World War II) the children's magazine, *La Semaine de Suzette* (Suzette's Week), was published on a weekly basis. The magazine included stories, games, crafts, recipes, instruction in the social graces and clothing patterns for Bleuette.

Bleuette was "born" in 1905, near the end of the hey-day of French dollmaking, just after Emile Jumeau and other makers of fine dolls in France bonded together to form the SFBJ (*Société Française de Fabrication de Bébés & Jouets*). Unlike the earlier French luxury dolls, Bleuette was created for interactive play, and as a teaching tool. She was conceived as the premium for the girls' magazine, *La Semaine de Suzette*, which was frankly promoting the values of the Roman Catholic Church at a time when France was becoming increasingly secular. Bleuette's mission was to help instruct little girls in the fine art of homemaking. From the very beginning, Bleuette seemed to invite her young owners into her own world, where girls could learn to become proper French ladies through play.

In order to increase interest in the doll and the new magazine, the publishers placed a unique emphasis on the wardrobe to be assembled for Bleuette. Patterns were offered frequently in the magazine. In 1916, the

Author's Note: Some years ago, a friend said: "Bleuette is an acquired taste." My hope is that all who read this book will be fortunate enough to acquire the taste for this unique little doll.

This dark-haired Première Bleuette is dressed in a Gautier-Languereau costume called "Simplet." She is marked "2" on her head, which has the typical steeply angled head cut used on dolls made by the Jumeau doll company. At the time the Première was made, the Jumeau doll company had become part of the SFBJ doll and toymaking cooperative formed by several different French dollmaking firms in 1899. The shoes are very old, but are not Bleuette shoes. She has blue eyes and a brown mohair wig.

An outstanding example of the Première Bleuette was part of the well-organized special exhibition, "Bécassine, Bleuette et les Poupées of La Semaine de Suzette," held from October 5, 1999 to February 27, 2000 at the Musée de la Poupée in Paris. Pictured with Bleuette is a silk-covered hat box, an embroidered felt purse, and a beguiling feather-trimmed bonnet, all made from patterns published in La Semaine de Suzette. Bleuette wears "Jolie robe" made by Suzanne Gautrot from a pattern published in the magazine in 1905. The exhibition was arranged by Samy Odin, Director of the Musée de la Poupée, and his father, Guido Odin, painter, photographer and costume master.

publishers of *La Semaine de Suzette* began offering a collection of beautifully sewn, commercial clothing for the doll twice a year. The brilliance of this approach to selling Bleuette and *La Semaine de Suzette* to French girls is demonstrated by the fact that all 20,000 dolls ordered by the publisher, Henri Gautier, in 1905 had been sold before the first issue of the magazine was published.

Bleuette's new "mama" was urged to begin sewing for her immediately. Over the years, if a child or her seamstress had made up every pattern published for Bleuette in the issues of *La Semaine de Suzette* and other publications of Gautier-Languereau, she would have needed several large trunks in which to store all the items! There were more than 1,060 patterns published over the fifty-five years Bleuette was produced. Many of the patterns had pieces and instructions for the making of multiple items. These patterns are an excellent window into the world of little girls during the decades between 1905 and 1960.

Bleuette's wardrobe needs were very similar to those of her owner. She needed school dresses, sturdy dresses for play, fancy party dresses and outfits for the varied sports in which she participated. Each outfit then required the necessary accoutrements to be complete—hats, stockings, belts, undergarments, outer wear, additional collars and cuffs (in case the first ones became soiled) and a host of aprons to protect her garments during Bleuette's busy days. One of the most charming aspects of Bleuette's life is that she was a very active child—always on the go, seeking new adventures, experiences and friends. Contemporary women seem to be responding to the excitement of her life and the wardrobe it required, just as little French girls did many years ago.

Bleuette was one of the first dolls to have outfits with slacks, as well as sports costumes that encouraged little girls to be active in boating, fencing, tennis and swimming. She even had an elegant pilot's costume for the new, promising field of aviation. The spiritual side of life was honored by the many First Communion costumes that were presented in the pages of *La Semaine de*

Suzette and the catalogs published by Gautier-Langeureau. Just as the children in each era learned about appropriate dress for every occasion, we today are able to catch a glimpse of the way life was lived in those decades.

Throughout history, the lives of ordinary women and children have been under-reported and studied. The study of toys offers a rare view of the perception of the roles of women and children in any particular era. Dolls, for their part, reflect how parents and society prepared little girls for their adult roles as wives and mothers.

From the very beginning, Bleuette has been associated with a large and stylish wardrobe. This lucky Bleuette, circa 1940, is standing amidst her wonderful trousseau, artfully displayed in a trunk for safekeeping. The doll is marked "71 Unis France 149 301," with a 1½ on the neck and the number 2 on her back. She has pierced ears and a brunette human-hair wig. She is 29 centimeters high.

Bleuette is an appropriate doll for serious study. Her fifty-year written history, with its continuous emphasis on her extensive wardrobe of *haute-couture* costumes, presents one view of social history over five decades. This remarkable doll survived two devastating world wars and the resulting deprivations at every level of life. Her ever-changing wardrobe needs mirrored the fluctuations of a rapidly changing society, especially following these two wars. What's more, unlike many other dolls, Bleuette's face and even her height, changed over the fifty-five years of her production. Thus, identification of authentic Bleuettes and their clothing takes careful study and attention to detail. Likewise, identifying the clothing sold by Gautier-Languereau requires additional study. For the doll connoisseur, the search for authenticity in Bleuette dolls and clothing is a challenging and exciting opportunity. For all doll collectors, Bleuette is a unique connection to several generations of little French girls, who acquired both a French sense of style and the pleasures of womanly graces through playing with this emblematic doll.

PART I THE DOLL

The dolls shown on these pages are described on page 175.

CHAPTER

1

A HISTORICAL PERSPECTIVE

In order to understand a phenomenon like Bleuette, it is important to place the doll and her story in the context of her own time. The start of the twentieth century had brought with it significant changes all over the world. Although many of these changes did not directly affect the introduction of Bleuette and her subsequent success, these events did re-shape the attitudes and philosophy of people in the new century, especially as pertaining to the proper way to rear young children. A brief overview of life in Europe and the United States, as well as in France, in the early years of the twentieth century may help the reader to understand the dynamics of this unique era.

Queen Victoria had died in England in 1901, ending an era that had an impact on daily lives on the Continent and in the United States, as well as in England. That same year, ragtime jazz music was developed in the United States; in Europe, Rachmaninoff's "Concerto #2" was played in concert halls for the first time. Enrico Caruso made his first phonograph recording. In 1902, Beatrix Potter's Peter Rabbit stories were published. Two years later J. M. Barrie's play entitled *Peter Pan* was first produced. Painters such as the French Claude Monet and the American John Singer Sargent were changing the way we looked at light.

This Première
Bleuette wears an
ensemble made by Suzanne
Gautrot, author of Nous Habillons
Bleuette, 1905-1922. *It consists of a*
red wool jacket with its wide white collar
and a navy pleated skirt attached to a white
muslin bodice. This manner of constructing
a skirt for a small doll was used frequently
in the ready-made clothing for
Bleuette, as well as in the patterns
in La Semaine de Suzette.

In 1903, Jack London published *The Call of the Wild* just as the Alaskan frontier was settled. Other events of 1903 that still have an amazing influence on our lives include the first flight of a powered airplane by brothers Orville and Wilbur Wright, the founding of the Ford Motor Company in Detroit, Michigan, the first coast-to-coast car trip in America, the creation of the first teddy bear, and the playing of the first post-season baseball game. France was undergoing a political shift towards a policy of separation of church and state. The election of Pope Pius X, who immediately called for a return to the more traditional church, fueled the anti-clerical feeling in France. The resulting tensions between the Vatican and the French government helped set the stage for Bleuette's birth.

By 1904, a ten-hour workday had been established in France. Steerage rates to the United States on foreign steamships were cut to $10 per person. In 1905, the Rotary Club was founded, neon lights were invented, the first motorbuses were introduced in London, rayon yarn was invented and Albert Einstein announced his Theory of Relativity. Franz Lehár wrote the "Merry Widow" in Vienna, and Claude Debussy wrote "La Mer" in Paris. Picasso had entered his "pink period" in painting and Henri Rousseau painted "Jungle with a Lion." The provinces of Alberta and Saskatchewan were formed in Canada. The first workers' "Soviet" was formed in St. Petersburg, Russia. In 1909, Louis Blériot flew an airplane across the English Channel, while English aviator Henri Farman completed the first one-hundred-mile flight. The age of plastics had a small beginning with the introduction of the first Bakelite products. Henri Matisse painted "The Dance" in France, and Frank Lloyd Wright built the Robie house in Chicago, Illinois. Robert E. Peary reached the North Pole. By 1911, the first film studio had been established in Hollywood, California. The following year, the Olympic decathlon and pentathlon medals were awarded to American Indian Jim Thorpe. This brief sampling of events in the first decade of the twentieth century serves to remind us of the vast and rapid changes occurring in society in Europe, as well as in the United States.

In the beginning of the twentieth century, the

Germans were rapidly overtaking the French as the dominant makers of toys in Europe. This shift to German supremacy in the manufacture of toys received a large boost when Solomon Fleischmann, a powerful German industrialist, became part of the French toymaking federation, *Société Français des Fabrication de Bébés et Jouets* (SFBJ) in 1899. German methods of production and competition were soon adopted at the SFBJ factory, resulting in "a decline in beauty and quality in the products."[1]

A number of economic factors influenced the decline of the doll and toy industry in France, while their German counterparts flourished. The two countries had very different approaches to creating successful business ventures. The German industrial complex was based on innovation and invention, and had access to ready credit from the banks, while the French depended on a more conservative approach and were reluctant to risk capital on new ideas. Compounding the problems for France, transportation of goods cost a great deal more in France than in Germany. Further complicating the picture, Germany had a very different view on how to distribute its goods. German companies printed illustrated catalogs and sent them all over the world in advance of sending salesmen out to take orders. The French sent out only a few salesmen and all actual orders had to be placed in France. The French preferred to have customers come to their numerous showrooms in Paris. In the meantime, the German toy and doll industry was efficiently taking orders, offering ease of payment and prompt delivery of goods. As Europe became increasingly industrialized, the French, always known for the beauty and fine quality of their products, did not adjust quickly enough to supply products to the world.[2]

Two devastating world wars were fought on French and German soil as these two nations with very different philosophies attempted to find a lasting peace. Although Bleuette survived these tumultuous times,

Among the many events of 1903 that still influence our lives was the introduction of the first teddy bear. Three very early teddy bears made by the German company Maragarete Steiff GmbH are, from left: an 18-inch golden bear, circa 1905; a 15-inch bear, circa 1904 and a grey 1905 11½ inch bear.

Even after the separation of church and state in 1904, the First Communion remained an important occasion in French girls' lives, as evidenced by the special dresses shown in the 1916 issue of the fashion magazine Le Petit Echo de la Mode.

the world into which she had been introduced in 1905 changed forever.

Earlier, in 1899, Emile Loubet had become the seventh president of the Third Republic in France. Under his leadership, various democratic reforms resulted in the establishment of obligatory secular education, along with freedom of assembly and the press. The French anti-Masonic newspaper, *Les Veillées des Chaumières* (Evenings in Country Cottages), wrote in opposition to the anti-clerical stance of the government.[3] In an article published on December 14, 1904, the paper asked, "Who will take the side of the Christian child, regardless of the struggle to be waged against the masonic press?" In answer to that question, the article went on to state, "Who?......A valiant little review that we are currently launching, to be ready for battle on February 1." This children's review—especially designed for young girls, the future mothers of France—was to include everything that might possibly interest the budding minds of girls between ages eight—thirteen.[4] Thus, the stage was set for the publication of *La Semaine de Suzette* in early 1905. Indeed, the premium doll for this new magazine was intended from the start as an aid to "fashion" the character of little French girls.

The law establishing the separation of church and state was presented in 1904 by Emile Combes, president of the French Cabinet, who was in charge of the Ministry of Interior and the Directorate of Religious Sects. This new law forbade any member of any religious community to teach at any level in the schools. These major political changes were directly involved in the introduction of *La Semaine de Suzette*, and the selection of its premium doll, Bleuette. As schools became more secular, educators continued to believe in the "usefulness of play as natural training in the republican values (girls) would need as the future wives and mothers of citizens."[5] Bleuette and *La Semaine de Suzette* carried this concept a step further in serving as a means to expound a moral doctrine steeped in Catholicism. But *La Semaine de Suzette* was not the first magazine designed to influence and educate little girls. In fact, children's literary publications had a long successful history in France prior to its appearance. In order to fully understand the success of Bleuette and *La Semaine de Suzette*, it is helpful to review these earlier magazines.

An important purpose behind the publication of La Semaine de Suzette *was to instill the values and teachings of the Roman Catholic Church in little French girls. As a result, many First Communion costumes were presented in the catalogs of Gautier-Languereau. Various activities associated with a young girl's First Communion, or Beau Jour, were discussed repeatedly in the pages of* La Semaine de Suzette. *Readers were encouraged to play out the rituals of that special day.*

2

CHILDREN'S MAGAZINES IN FRANCE

The publication of magazines just for children
had a strong tradition in France. An impres-
sive number of publications were designed to
capture the imaginations of children. We can go back
as far as 1833, to the publication of *Magasin des
Demoiselles*, which enjoyed some success, in spite of its
small format. That editor's mistaken thinking was that
small girls would prefer a small-format magazine.
Journal des Demoiselles, which was published at the same
time, used a larger format, the same as that used in
women's fashion magazines, which was far more popular among young girls. (When *La Semaine de Suzette*
came on the scene, the publishers showed they had
learned the lesson from their predecessors by printing
their new publication in the larger format.)

In 1863, the *Journal des Demoiselles* hired Mademoiselle
Jeanne Peronne to help develop a new magazine: *La
Poupée Modèle*. Mlle. Peronne had opened a doll shop
near the offices of the *Journal des Demoiselles*. She is
credited with creating the concept of naming a doll
to be used as a "connecting link" between issues of
the magazine. Mlle. Peronne named the doll for *La
Poupée Modèle* Lily. Although she sold only Lily dolls
in her shop, she offered these dolls made to various
specifications, at different prices. She then used the
name Lily to refer to whatever doll the little readers

*Opposite page: The fascination
with the future roles of little girls
as the "mothers of France" led to
an unprecedented interest in dolls.
This November 1886 issue of this
elegantly illustrated magazine,* La
Mode Illustrée, *offered a full page
devoted to various types of dolls,
their necessary clothing, and
accessories. Learning how to dress
appropriately through doll
costuming had a long, rich history
in France, even before Bleuette and
La Semaine de Suzette were
introduced.*

bon sur la poste et en y ajou-
tant 1 franc pour les frais d'ex-
pédition en France, et 3 francs
pour l'étranger.

Tablette
ORNÉE DE BRODERIE.

La figure 36 (recto) du supplément appartient à cet objet.

La tablette est en porcelaine
blanche ; sa hauteur est de
23 centimètres, sa largeur, de
13 centimètres; un morceau de
cuir orné de broderies s'y rat-
tache. La tablette est en outre
fixée dans un cadre recouvert
en peluche olive, qui peut être
suspendu ou posé debout au
moyen d'un morceau de carton
fixé sur la paroi du dos. La
broderie est exécutée sur du
cuir olive clair avec de la soie
olive foncé et des fils d'or; on
reporte le dessin, d'après la
figure 36, sur le cuir; on troue
les contours à intervalles régu-

Toilette pour poupée.

Tablette ornée de broderie.

liers, et l'on passe dans les
trous un brin de cordonnet d'or
retenu par des points transversaux en soie olive foncé. Le
fond se trouvant entre les contours est orné avec des points
allongés en soie olive. On at-
tache à l'anneau servant à sus-
pendre la tablette une cordelière en soie ter-
minée par un petit gland.

Jupon de poupée.

Ce jupon est fait avec de la laine blanche, au
crochet, en un dessin à côtes se composant de
mailles simples; son bord inférieur est garni
d'une rangée de dents; son bord supérieur est
garni d'un tour de brides. La fente est bordée
de mailles-chaînettes simples. On commence le
jupon par le bord supérieur en faisant une chaînette de 55 mailles sur lesquelles on fait en
allant et en revenant :

1er tour. — On passe la plus proche maille,
— * 2 mailles simples sur les
2 plus proches mailles, — 3 mailles simples sur la maille
suivante, — 2 mailles simples sur les 2 plus proches
mailles, — 2 mailles simples sur les 2 mailles suivantes,
en terminant ensemble les côtés de mailles supérieurs
de ces mailles; on recommence encore 7 fois depuis *,
mais à la dernière répétition, on laisse sans les faire les
2 dernières mailles terminées ensemble.

2e tour. — Une maille en l'air, — * 3
mailles simples sur les 3 plus proches
mailles (en piquant toujours sur le côté
de maille par derrière), — 3 mailles simples sur la maille suivante, — 3 mailles
simples sur les 3 plus proches mailles,
— on passe une maille; on recommence
encore 7 fois depuis *.

3e au 43e tour. — Comme le tour précédent, mais dans chaque tour suivant,
à l'exception des 10e et 12e tours, on
passe toujours 2 mailles au lieu d'une, et
le nombre des mailles simples de chaque division du dessin s'augmente d'une
maille après l'exécution de chacun des
tours désignés. On assemble les bords transversaux à
l'envers au moyen de mailles simples, on laisse sans
les réunir 5 côtés au bord supérieur, pour former la
fente, et l'on fait au bord inférieur, pour la rangée
de dents : * une maille simple sur la plus proche
maille, — 4 brides sur la
2e maille suivante, — on
passe une maille; on re-
commence depuis *, — en
terminant, une maille-
chaînette simple sur la 1re
maille simple de ce tour.
On fait au bord supérieur
toujours une bride sur
chaque maille de la chaî-
nette, et à la fente, toujours 2 mailles-chaînettes
simples sur chaque maille
de lisière.

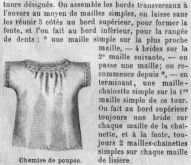

Costume de poupée
au crochet.

Nº 1.   Nº 2.
Capotes pour poupées.

Guêtre
pour poupée.

Toque   Béret
pour poupées.

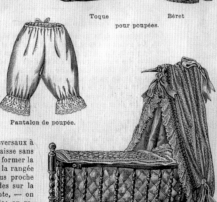

Pantalon de poupée.

Berceau de poupée.

Chemise de poupée.

Béret de poupée.

Ce béret est fait au crochet
avec de la laine zéphyr bleue,
en un dessin de mailles simples.
Le milieu est orné d'un pom-
pon en laine semblable. On le
commence depuis le milieu par
une chaînette de 4 mailles en
l'air dont on joint la dernière
à la première, en l'on fait le

1er tour. — 7 mailles simples
sur le rond.

2e tour. — Toujours 2 mailles
simples sur chaque maille (l'en-
droit de l'ouvrage forme l'envers du béret).

3e tour. — 7 fois alternativement, pour une augmenta-
tion, 2 mailles simples sur la plus
proche maille, une maille simple sur la maille suivante.

4e au 12e tour. — Comme le
tour précédent, mais on augmente le nombre des mailles
simples, d'une maille simple
entre chaque 2 augmentations,
dans chaque tour suivant.

13e tour. — Toujours une

Costume de poupée.

maille simple sur chaque maille,
mais on termine ensemble les
6 mailles au-dessus de chaque
augmentation.

14e tour. — Toujours une
maille simple sur chaque maille,
mais on termine ensemble les
4 mailles au-dessus de chaque
diminution du tour précédent. — On fait encore 4 tours de mailles simples en conservant
le même nombre de mailles, et les faisant toujours sur deux côtés de mailles.

Costume de poupée au crochet.

Le costume de cette poupée se compose d'un
pantalon, d'une blouse de matelot et d'un béret;
on le fait avec de la laine bleue et blanche, en
un dessin de mailles simples.

Pantalon. On fait d'abord avec de la laine
bleue, pour chaque moitié du pantalon, depuis
le bord inférieur, une chaînette de 18 mailles
dont on joint la dernière à la première, et sur
laquelle on fait 18 tours de mailles simples,
toujours une maille simple sur
chaque maille; on pique le crochet depuis le 2e tour, toujours
sur 2 côtés de mailles; on aug-
mente d'une maille au commencement de chaque tour
depuis le 6e jusqu'au 18e tour. Lorsque les deux moitiés
sont terminées, on les réunit avec une maille simple et
l'on fait sur toutes les mailles
en rond, encore 18 tours; dans
le dernier de ces tours, on fait
toujours alternativement 2 mailles simples sur les 2 plus proches mailles et l'on passe la
maille suivante. On passe dans
les mailles du dernier tour une
petite cordelière pour mainte-
nir le pantalon.

On commence la blouse avec
de la laine blanche, depuis le
milieu de devant, par une chaînette de 23 mailles, et l'on fait
toujours en allant, jusqu'à la

Costume de ville
pour poupée.

moitié, 34 tours de mailles simples dont les 5e et 6e
tours sont faits avec de la laine bleue; on a fait en
raccourcissant les 11e et 12e, 15e et 16e, 19e et 20e,
23e et 24e tours, ainsi que les 27e et 28e tours (formant
les tours intercalés); on fait chaque fois le 1er des
2 tours indiqués sur les
11 mailles simples se trouvant le plus près du bord
inférieur; le 2e de ces tours
est fait sur les 15 mailles
simples se trouvant le plus
près du bord inférieur. Il
faut remarquer que, dans
le 17e jusqu'au 22e tour,
on laisse sans les faire les
6 mailles se trouvant le
plus près du bord supé-
rieur, pour former l'en-
tournure, et à la fin du
22e tour, on pose 6 nou-

Robe au crochet
pour poupée.

Mon Journal *captured a delighted audience of young readers with its artfully drawn, colorful illustrations. This children's magazine was typical of French publications of the day: it was published on newsprint paper and printed in a small format, measuring just 6-1/2 by 10 inches. Only the front and back covers were printed in color. The inside illustrations were lithographs—which seemed to invite many of the young readers to add a touch of color with their crayons! This magazine featured serialized stories, games and patterns for making doll clothing.*

chose to costume with the patterns from the magazine. *La Poupée Modèle* was published until 1924.

From the first issue, Lily was part of *La Poupée Modèle*. She was a fairly large doll—45 centimeters tall (17-1/2 inches), which happened to be the ideal size for a doll as stated by the celebrated Parisian dollmaker Mlle. Calixte Huret, who felt a doll should be one-third the height of the child owner.[6] Lily was soon followed by a smaller boy doll named Benjamin—just as Bleuette eventually had her own "family" in *La Semaine de Suzette*.

In the early years of the twentieth century a small-format magazine, *Mon Journal*, featuring beautiful color artwork, was also published for children. A premium doll was offered, and the magazine provided patterns in a section called: *"Modes de Poupée."*

Other French children's magazines included *Le Journal de la Jeunesse* (the Journal of Youth), *Le Petit Français illustré* (The Illustrated Little Frenchman) and *L'Écolier illustré* (The Illustrated Schoolboy). *La Jeune Fille du XX siècle* (The Young Girl of the Twentieth Century) was published from 1902 to 1905.[7] Several of these magazines featured patterns appropriate for child seamstresses to use to costume their dolls. However, Henri Gautier was the first publisher to combine the selling of a doll, Bleuette, with patterns specifically designed just for this doll, through advertisements in his magazine, *La Semaine de Suzette*, and entire catalogs of clothing after 1916.

Let's look at the background of the publication of *La Semaine de Suzette* itself. In 1877, a Socialist newspaper, *L'Ouvrier* (The Worker), announced the forthcoming publication of *Les Veillées des Chaumieres* (Evenings in Country Cottages). While *L'Ouvrier* eventually disappeared, *Les Veillées des Chaumieres* grew. The managing director was Charles Bleriot. Soon, Henri Gautier joined Bleriot in publishing *Les Veillées*. Before *La Semaine de Suzette* was published in 1905, Henri Gautier became sole publisher of *Les Veillées*. In 1918, Gautier invited his nephew, Maurice Langeureau, to join the firm. The publishing firm has been known as Gautier-Langeureau since 1918. (Gautier-Langeureau is now a part of the publishing company Hachette Livre in France, which continues to re-issue books in the Bécassine series. Hachette Livre retains copyrights associated with their purchase

of Gautier-Languereau Publishing.)

Henri Gautier was concerned with the problem of the void left in teaching when the religious sects were barred from the schools. He addressed this problem through publication of a magazine for little girls. The content of this new magazine was intended to instill in the readers the values of being good mothers and wives, and to teach these future mothers of France how to create a beautiful home and to acquire the skills of sewing and needlework. He chose to accomplish all this through stories, articles, craft projects and patterns for a stylish wardrobe for the premium doll, Bleuette, which he offered to subscribers of the magazine.

Long before the publication of the first issue of *La Semaine de Suzette*, Gautier called together his editorial staff to design the proposed new magazine. Among those invited to participate was Madame Bernard de Laroche, who was a writer for *Les Veillées des Chaumières*. Her writing focus was primarily young women and girls. She wrote under the pen name of Jacqueline Rivière—a name that would soon be familiar to all girls who read *La Semaine de Suzette*. She appears to have been in charge of developing Bleuette and her fashionably-styled wardrobe.

When Gautier decided to offer a doll as a premium to encourage little girls to subscribe to his new magazine, he showed a remarkably modern marketing genius and a thorough understanding of little girls. He knew that daughters of the *bourgeois* (middle class) at this time owned a "personal" doll. This was a custom that was first popularized by *La Poupée Modèle* through their mascot doll, Lily. When Gautier decided to offer a doll as premium, he may well have turned to Mme. Laroche, who was the mother of a young daughter. The suggestion to use a small, size 2 Jumeau doll for the new magazine's premium may well have come from Mme. Laroche.[8]

Bleuette was offered "free," for a year's subscription to *La Semaine de Suzette*. The doll could also be purchased for 2.50 francs with the purchase of a single issue of the magazine. Gautier's final marketing ploy was to offer the first issue of the magazine free at newsstands. His strategy obviously worked. By almost any standards, the magazine and its mascot doll were a great

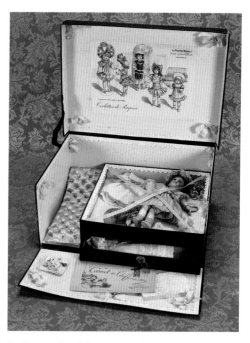

La Poupée Modèle *was a girls' magazine especially associated with dolls and patterns from 1890 to 1924. The primary doll used as the model for the patterns published in this magazine was Lily, a 45-centimeter doll sold by the editor of the magazine in her doll shop. Dolls of other sizes were sold in the shop as well. Instructions were given with the patterns for enlarging or shrinking the pattern pieces to fit dolls of specific sizes. In this lovely presentation called an Etrenne, circa 1905, a Simon & Halbig 1078 bisque-headed doll on a wood-and-composition jointed body was offered with trousseau, and even a tufted satin bed. She was named Chiffonette. The inside of the lid features an illustration from* La Poupée Modèle, July 1905. *This set was described as "the doll from* La Poupée Modèle."

Quatrième Année. — N° 140. Dimanche 16 Mars 1924.

16 Pages

Lisette

PRIX: 20 Centimes

Paraît : Chaque Semaine.

Journal des Petites Filles

BUREAUX : 1, rue Gazan, PARIS (XIVe) R. C. Seine 53879.

caption could go here
Colette Yay

PAUVRE TOMMY

(Voir l'histoire pages 8 et 9.)

success. Before the first issue of the magazine, dated February 2, 1905, could be delivered, the original 20,000 dolls ordered by Gautier had been given out as premiums for subscriptions. In the August 1906 issue, the magazine announced there were 80,000 subscribers.[9]

Sixteen years after the first issue of *La Semaine de Suzette* was published, in 1921, a new magazine called *Lisette* appeared. It featured a slightly smaller format than *La Semaine de Suzette*, but in most other aspects, *Lisette* copied the successful formula of the earlier magazine. In each issue of *Lisette*, there were stories, games, sewing lessons, menus and patterns for making a doll wardrobe. A lovely doll named Lisette was offered as a premium for subscribing to the magazine. Lisette was first offered with a porcelain head; she had glass eyes, wore a simple chemise, and came in either a blonde or brunette hair color. She was 33 centimeters tall (13 inches) on a fully articulated composition body. (In 1923, she was made available with a composition head.) In 1922, the magazine also offered premiums of a white metal beaded purse or a bed for Lisette, in addition to the doll. Many patterns for Lisette were published over the years, resulting in a very complete wardrobe. The instructions and pattern piece diagrams were somewhat simpler to follow than those for Bleuette in *La Semaine de Suzette*. There appears to have been a conscious effort in *Lisette* to provide patterns that closely resembled those for Bleuette and, in spite of the difference in the size of the dolls, many of the patterns for Lisette also fit Bleuette. This magazine was almost as popular as *La Semaine de Suzette*, and was published for fifty-two years.

The only other children's magazine that was published for as long as *La Semaine de Suzette* was *Filette*, which also lasted fifty-five years. The first issue of *Filette* was published in 1909.[10]

Although the United States did not have a girls' magazine, *per se*, in 1900 a women's publication, *Ladies Home Journal*, was introduced that also used a doll and patterns to entice new subscribers. While the magazine was written for adults, its editors certainly aimed

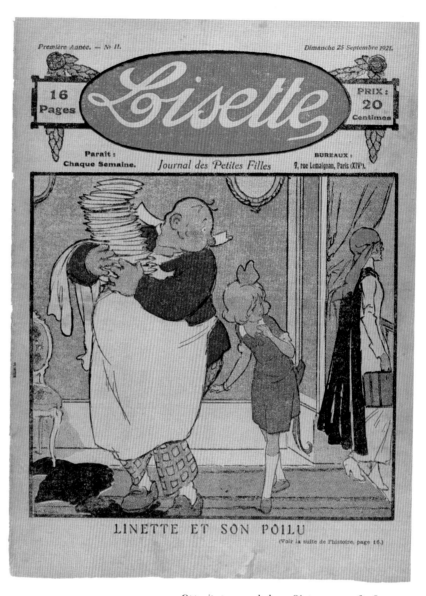

Opposite page and above: Sixteen years after La Semaine de Suzette *began delighting young girls, another magazine was introduced:* Lisette. *The two magazines have a very similar look, and both offered a lovely mascot doll. Patterns for making the doll's wardrobe appeared in both magazines, and the costumes were remarkably similar. The mascot doll for* Lisette *was 33 centimeters tall (13 inches). Even so, the bodies were similar enough that when the 29-centimeter Bleuette was introduced, patterns from either magazine (except for tightly fitted clothing) could be made to fit either mascot doll.*

to encourage girls to read its pages by including charming paper dolls of a wealthy extended family and their servants, drawn by Sheila Young. In 1911 the Lettie Lane family included a doll named Daisy. The paper-doll feature was quite popular, and led to the magazine offering a real doll version of Daisy, advertising her as "the doll who came to life." The bisque-headed, German-made Daisy was a premium offered to little girls who sold three yearly paid subscriptions to *Ladies Home Journal*. Patterns could be ordered to make Daisy an extensive wardrobe.

The *Ladies Home Journal* also had a somewhat political agenda: articles and stories were designed to reassure homemakers of the properness of their traditional roles.[11] This sentiment echoes the French concern of the same era that the traditional role of women might disappear due to the separation of church and state, and especially that girls would not learn the importance of these traditional roles if the Catholic Church were barred from providing school teachers.

Bleuette was not the only doll offered as a premium by a magazine in the first half of the twentieth century. Needlecraft Magazine, *published in the United States, offered this chubby-cheeked doll for four subscriptions. For an additional two subscriptions, the child could order a little dress and romper.*

Below: These Bleuettes are gathered at the home of Suzanne Gautrot in Paris. From left: the costumes are "Milles raies," from summer 1939; "Double emploi," from summer 1950; "Lavendeau," from winter 1938-1939; and a dress made by Suzanne Gautrot from La Semaine de Suzette, *issue 10, 1957.*

Opposite page: In the United States in 1911, the Ladies Home Journal *offered little girls a doll named* Daisy *as a premium for selling subscriptions. The jointed doll with a porcelain head and composition body doll was based on a beautiful paper doll of the same name, which was a regular feature in the magazine. Daisy became so popular that the magazine had to order dolls from more than one company. The 17- or 18-inch Daisy was marked either as a Kestner 171, or with had a head made by Simon & Halbig on a body by H. Handwerck. Patterns for underwear and clothing were sent free with each doll. This example is an all-original Kestner 171 Daisy. She came dressed in a simple muslin frock.*

3

LA SEMAINE DE SUZETTE

L *a Semaine de Suzette* was published weekly until 1914. That year, following issue #30 (numbering of the issues started anew with #1 each year), shortages caused by the war effort forced changes in the publication schedule. Two special combined issues were produced in 1914: #31-36 and #37-42. The normal publishing schedule resumed with issue #43 that year.

During the war years, little girls were encouraged to have Bleuette "give up her turn to our soldiers." Instead of sewing or knitting for their dolls, girls were urged to work for the soldiers instead. That a magazine for children would refer so specifically to serious international events—and even request that the readers play a small part in them—demonstrates quite clearly the changing view of children's place in society by 1914.

The war and the resulting shortages it caused were reflected in the price of Bleuette. Until 1915, Bleuette was sold at her introductory price of 2.50 French francs. From 1915 to 1918, the price rose to 3 FF. After the war, the price jumped to 7.50 FF.

Anti-German sentiment also found its way into the pages of *La Semaine de Suzette*. The publisher proudly reminded girls that their precious Bleuettes were "born in Paris of French parents (I mean makers)." (*LSdS*,

Opposite page: Henri Gautier began publishing La Semaine de Suzette *on February 2, 1905. Shown here is the cover of the March 16, 1905 issue. The magazines featured colorful artwork and a large format, similar to the magazines published for women at the time.*

PREMIÈRE-ANNÉE. N° 7. 16 MARS 1905.

LA SEMAINE DE SUZETTE

PUBLICATION POUR LA JEUNESSE PARAISSANT LE JEUDI

ABONNEMENT d'un an : France, Algérie, Belgique. . . . 6 fr. | Autres colonies et pays étrangers. 8 fr.

Le numéro : **10 centimes**.

BUREAUX ET ADMINISTRATION : 55, Quai des Grands-Augustins, 55, à Paris.

CONCOURS DE LA CORBEILLE RENVERSÉE (Premier tableau)

Cherchez les dés. (Voir l'explication et les conditions du concours, page 110.)

Issue 51, 1917) The writer went on to proclaim that there is "no need for a single French child to have a German-made toy in her hands." (*LSdS*, Issue 51) But the fact is that early in Bleuette's production (during the time Solomon Fleischmann was at the helm of SFBJ), the charming 6/0 doll had a head imported from Germany.[12]

With the onset of the Second World War, Gautier-Languereau Publishing was forced to suspend publication of *La Semaine de Suzette* in June 1940. Regular publication would not resume until May 1946—a hiatus of six long, traumatic years in the lives of French children. When regular printing began again, the magazine was published every two months, until October, when a normal printing schedule was resumed.[13]

The production of Bleuette, her baby brother Bambino, and their charming wardrobes also resumed

The magazine, La Semaine de Suzette, *could be purchased in individual copies or could be delivered direct to the house via a subscription. The magazines were also available at the end of the year in a bound volume, such as pictured here. Some families who subscribed chose to simply take their magazines to a bindery where the issues were organized and protected in a plain, hard-cover binding. Girls often created their own little* La Semaine *books by cutting holes along the left edge of their magazines, then running colorful yarn or string through the holes. This helped keep the issues for a half year together. These magazines were referred to over and over, as is attested to by the condition in which we now find early editions.*

in 1946. However, a shortage of materials soon caused production to stop until the spring of 1948. In issue #4, in 1947, the young readers were asked to be patient. Fabrics were in short supply, especially fine materials like those formerly used for Bleuette's trousseau.

Although publication of the catalogs had also resumed, some of the ensembles pictured were never made as depicted. *La Semaine de Suzette* informed girls that the beautiful clothing offered by Gautier-Languereau continued to be designed by Madame Languereau, who had drawn all the costumes for Bleuette for many years. The patterns published in *La Semaine de Suzette* were a different matter; they were drawn by a person identified as "Doty."

Patterns to make lovely, rather complex, costumes for Bleuette had been part of *La Semaine de Suzette* from its inception. Discussions and some instructions for each pattern were written by "Tante Jacqueline." The early patterns followed the finest fashions of the day, echoing the latest styles for upper-middle-class little girls. Very little accommodation was made for the fact that young children were expected to sew from these advanced patterns! One suspects that mothers, nursemaids, and household seamstresses were often called upon to create the beautiful dresses and hats.

Just as there was variation in the Bleuette doll, the patterns in *La Semaine de Suzette* also changed over time. Because patterns to make new ensembles were drawn in the most current fashions of each season, Bleuette's wardrobe is an excellent research tool for studying the evolution of children's clothing during the years 1905–1960. (The patterns will be discussed in depth in chapter six.)

As the popularity of Bleuette increased, the firm of Gautier-Languereau began publishing colorful catalogs of beautifully made costumes for Bleuette twice a year. The firm sought skilled seamstresses to make ever more elaborate costumes, always *le dernier cri* (the latest styles of the day), for Bleuette. The clothing was designed, after 1918, by the wife of Maurice Languereau and sewn by experienced seamstresses. It is surmised that some of these ladies may have had regular jobs sewing for the great fashion houses, but wished to earn extra money by making the exquisite

A jolly clown graces the cover of the August 2, 1906 issue of La Semaine de Suzette. *It is easy to see why these charming magazines had immediate appeal to young girls.*

Although La Semaine de Suzette *was delivered to the homes of girls who subscribed, it was also sold in bound volumes containing issues from one-half of the year. Individual copies of the magazine were also privately bound, to aid in the preservation of all the issues for one year. Examples of both kinds of bound volumes, as well as the single issues of the magazine, are avidly sought by collectors today.*

The firm of Gautier-Languereau published many books during the same years they published La Semaine de Suzette. *One example is* Les Vacances de Suzette, *which was published in 1909. These small format books featured stories, scripts for little dramas, patterns, and word games—all the sorts of activities girls might have time to do while vacationing.*

A later version of the small books designed to suggest activities to girls who were on vacation is Suzette en Vacances, *published in 1955.*

doll clothes. Madame Languereau's friendship with Jeanne Lanvin, of the high-fashion House of Lanvin, helped ensure that the patterns created for Bleuette were on the cutting edge of fashion. Soon Bleuette's wardrobe not only echoed current trends; often it introduced new trends.

The clothing offered through the catalogs was quite different from what was usually offered as commercially made clothing for dolls. Not only were Bleuette's costumes at the absolute height of style and fashion, they were beautifully stitched and carefully finished, even on the inside of the garments. The fabrics were of excellent quality, rather than the inexpensive cloth commonly used for doll clothes. The closures were metal hooks; the buttons, belt buckles, braid and ribbon trim were all of the highest quality. Bleuette's shoes were made of the finest leathers and embossed on the sole with her initial. Her costumes came fully accessorized with hats, handbags, gloves or other necessary pieces. The publishers declared that "Bleuette will be a lesson of good taste for little girls."[14]

In addition to publishing *La Semaine de Suzette*, the publishing firm of Gautier-Languereau also published many fine books for children. Perhaps the most recognizable series is the one with Bécassine as the heroine. The series of books about this charming, funny nursemaid extraordinaire began in 1913. By 1950, twenty-seven different titles had been published. Even after the death of Pinchot, the original illustrator, Gautier-Languereau continued to produce Bécassine books with illustrations by Jean Trubert until 1962.[15] (Many of these delightful books are available today to a new generation of children through Hachette Livre, now the parent company of Gautier-Languereau.)

Gautier-Languereau also published a series of books for the holidays. The first, which appeared in 1906, was called *Prime de Vacances;* by 1909 it was called *Les Vacances de Suzette.* These charming books were filled with short stories, games, embroidery patterns, music, plays, crafts and recipes—all suitable for keeping young girls fully occupied during their school holidays.

From the earliest days, Gautier published lists of costumes available for Bleuette in *La Semaine de Suzette,* under the heading of *"Le Trousseau* de Bleuette." While the early examples simply listed accessories, clothing, lingerie and shoes available for purchase from M. Gautier, the intriguing names of the dresses suggest the world of high fashion in Paris. By 1912, graceful drawings of Bleuette in various ensembles accompanied the clothing advertisements. In 1914, a grainy photograph of Bleuette in a nursing costume accompanied a list of desirable gifts for Bleuette's Christmas list. The regular feature of *"Le Trousseau de Bleuette"* was thus well established before the publication of the individual catalogs of Bleuette costumes, which began with the Winter 1916-1917 issue.

The catalogs of clothing for Bleuette continued with a new edition published twice each year. The catalogs were beautifully illustrated by known illustrators, including Maggie Salcedo and Manon Lessel. Each ensemble was given a name designed to engage a child's imagination.

n fact, every issue of *La Semaine de Suzette* was created to enlarge a little girl's vision of the world around her. There were clever stories of the exploits of young girls, scripts for theatrical productions, poetry, music, science lessons and instruction about animals and wildlife. Recipes, crafts, games and puzzles were also included. Some of the stories were retellings of familiar fairy tales. Several stories involved charming mysteries, which were ultimately "solved" by young girls. Others were frankly geared to expanding the horizons of young readers. One such case is a romanticized story of the American Wild West, in which a farmer named Billy has a large ranch on the Great Plains, but no sons to help him with the work. Instead, he has two daughters, Noma and Sabra, who are thirteen and fifteen, and help him do the work of boys. The story continues in predictable fashion as the two sisters "save the day." Billy is very proud of the brave girls with their "spirit and courage."[16]

Of course, not all the stories were full of make-believe. The great people of the day were featured in articles, along with the significance of their achievements, such as: Madame Curie and her discovery of radium; pioneer aviator Michael Détroyat; Commander Maurice Rossi of the military forces; two early women aviators, Maryse Bastié and Maryse Hilsz; and a child prodigy named Gerard Singer. Many of

As the world changed, so did the artwork in La Semaine de Suzette. *This cover from the 1955 issue illustrates some of the changes in design. The remarkable feat of this little magazine is that it managed to evolve and change over time, always retaining the loyal support and interest of the young French girls.*

the articles and stories also told of diverse cultures all over the world. In 1938, a somber note was struck by the inclusion of a black-bordered death notice for M. Henri Gautier.

rom the beginning of its publication, *La Semaine de Suzette* demonstrated a changing viewpoint about Bleuette's identity, which creates some confusion for collectors today. The title of the magazine means, literally, Suzette's Week. Since the mascot doll was not named Suzette, how did Bleuette fit into Suzette's world, and vice versa? As with most questions regarding Bleuette, there is no simple, single answer.

In the first decade of publication, the magazine seemed to characterize Bleuette as the child reading the magazines. In these early issues, Bleuette even took care of her own doll, Mignonette. Patterns were given so Bleuette (and the child reader) could make small-scale furniture for the four-inch Mignonette, who was given to Bleuette for Christmas 1905.

Fifteen years later, without fanfare, the reader of *La Semaine de Suzette* was asked to imagine herself as

When a little girl was fortunate enough to shop for her Bleuette's new clothing at the Gautier-Languereau shop on rue Jacob in Paris, she would bring her purchases home in a stylish paper shopping bag provided by the store. The delightful designs on the bags were created by the same artists who designed the art for the catalogs.

Opposite page: In addition to the magazine, La Semaine de Suzette, *and the books, Gautier-Languereau also published two catalogs a year, beginning in 1916, featuring ready-made ensembles for Bleuette. These adorable costumes were always* haute couture *and very beautifully stitched. The catalogs are real collectors' items today; often selling for more than $100 at auction. This example is from 1925. Various well-known illustrators were hired by Gautier-Languereau to portray Bleuette's many fashions. This charming picture of Bleuette and her doll were created by "Colette," who drew Bleuette's fashions for several years.*

One of the most endearing and popular characters introduced in the pages of La Semaine de Suzette *was the nanny, Bécassine. Her story was told in numerous continuing comic book-style series in* La Semaine de Suzette. *This example of "Bécassine in the Snow," is typical of the stories published in* La Semaine de Suzette.

Suzette, and Bleuette took the role of a beloved doll who shares her owner's adventures, joys and sorrows. More furniture patterns were published in the magazine, but they were scaled for Bleuette, and the child reader was obviously being instructed to create the pieces for her doll. The furniture patterns offered for Mignonette were appropriate for the early 1900s. The larger furniture patterns published in the late 1920s were, at first, art nouveau, and later, art deco, in design. In these later years, Bleuette assumed her rightful place as a toy used to encourage little girls to learn the art and craft of sewing.[17]

Since a primary purpose of publishing *La Semaine de Suzette* was to teach little French girls various domestic arts for creating a comfortable home, the inclusion of recipes in the magazine should come as no surprise. However, the complexity of the recipes, and the fact that many required the use of wine or liquor is a bit more startling. There were many recipes for desserts and sweets, which frequently featured rich French chocolate among the ingredients. Perhaps as a natural adjunct, as early as 1906 a recipe for making toothpaste was also included! Recipes for *soufflés* and sauces were frequently offered, with suggestions to garnish with seasonally ripe fruits and vegetables. There were also recipes for tarts, jams and jam-filled pastries. In August 1906, the following recipe for cold lemonade was published, which had been sent in to the magazine by *Blondinette de Dunkerque.*

> *Cut and squeeze 5 lemons. Remove the seeds, then add 500 grams of sugar and 2 liters of boiling water. Allow to cool for a quarter of an hour. Serve well chilled.*

Opposite page: The Bécassine stories in the La Semaine de Suzette *led to a lively series of books featuring Bécassine as the heroine. The books were first published in 1913, and their publication has continued, even today, by Hachette Publishing, which owns the rights to Gautier-Languereau's publishing empire. This first volume, which tells the story of Bécassine's infancy and childhood, was illustrated by Joseph-Porphyre Pinchon.*

L'Enfance de BÉCASSINE

Henri GAUTIER, Éditeur
55, Quai des Grands-Augustins, PARIS

1936

ÉDITIONS GAUTIER-LANGUEREAU

R. C. Seine 15.995   **18, Rue Jacob, PARIS (6ᵉ)**   Ch. Post. 336-47

Albums et Livres illustrés pour les Enfants
Romans pour les Jeunes Gens et les Jeunes Filles
Collection historique "Scènes et Tableaux", ouvrages utiles, etc.

L'ALPHABET DE BÉCASSINE

Ces trois albums, format 22 x 32, sous couverture carton souple, sont entièrement illustrés en couleurs.

Le plus gai des alphabets; grâce à lui, l'heure de la lecture n'est plus une étude pour les petits, mais une récréation.

1 Album . . . . **7 fr.**

■

Textes de
CAUMERY

■

Illustrations de
J.-P. PINCHON

BÉCASSINE MAITRESSE D'ECOLE

Suite et complément de l'alphabet. Les tout-petits riront aux larmes des mésaventures de Bécassine, racontées en phrases courtes et de lecture facile.

1 Album . . . . **11 fr.**

LES CHANSONS DE BECASSINE

14 Chansons, piano et chant, toutes très drôles et faciles à apprendre. (Paroles de Charles Magué, d'après Caumery, musique de Fr. Darcieux.)

1 Album . . . **14 fr.**

LES ALBUMS DE BÉCASSINE

par CAUMERY.   Illustrations de J.-P. PINCHON

■

Nouveauté :

Bécassine à Clocher-les-Bécasses

Et voilà Bécassine revenue dans son pays natal pour y surveiller les réparations du château de Grand-Air qu'un étrange locataire, le nommé Rastaquouéros, a laissé en piteux état. A Clocher-les-Bécasses, Bécassine retrouve sa cousine la célèbre Marie Quillouch, mariée maintenant. Aidée de son peu scrupuleux époux, Marie a monté une machination par laquelle elle espère s'enrichir aux dépens de la pauvre marquise. Mais Bécassine veille, et aussi le bon oncle Corentin. Tout s'arrange grâce à eux, grâce plus encore à des péripéties imprévues qui ont inspiré à Caumery et Pinchon des textes et des dessins pleins d'esprit et de gaieté. Dans la riche série des albums de Bécassine, celui-ci comptera comme l'un des plus variés et des plus amusants.

Albums précédemment parus :

1. L'enfance de Bécassine
2. Bécassine en apprentissage
3. Bécassine pendant la guerre
4. Bécassine chez les Alliés
5. Bécassine mobilisée
6. Bécassine chez les Turcs
7. Les cent métiers de Bécassine
8. Bécassine voyage
9. Bécassine nourrice
10. Bécassine alpiniste
11. Les bonnes idées de Bécassine
12. Bécassine au Pays Basque
13. Bécassine, son oncle et leurs amis
14. L'automobile de Bécassine
15. Bécassine au pensionnat
16. Bécassine en aéroplane
17. Bécassine fait du scoutisme
18. Bécassine aux bains de mer
19. Bécassine dans la neige

20. Bécassine prend des pensionnaires.

Chaque Album, relié dos toile, contenant une histoire complète et pouvant être lu isolément, format 22 x 32, 64 pages entièrement illustrées en couleurs, sous couverture simili-aquarelle. . . . . **19 fr.**

Inside the 1936 book catalog, various editions of books featuring Bécassine as the heroine were described.

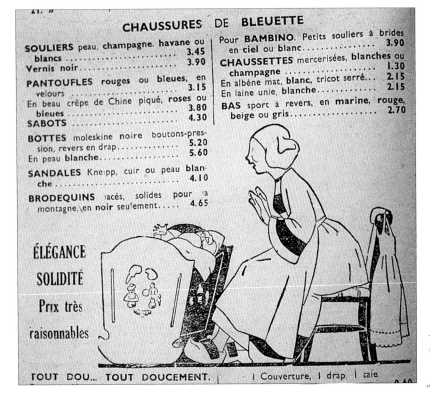

CHAUSSURES DE BLEUETTE

SOULIERS peau. champagne. havane ou blancs **3.45**
Vernis noir **3.90**

PANTOUFLES rouges ou bleues, en velours **3.15**
En beau crêpe de Chine piqué, roses ou bleues **3.80**
SABOTS **4.30**

BOTTES moleskine noire boutons-pression, revers en drap **5.20**
En peau blanche **5.60**

SANDALES Kneipp, cuir ou peau blanche **4.10**

BRODEQUINS lacés, solides pour la montagne, en noir seulement **4.65**

Pour **BAMBINO**. Petits souliers à brides en ciel ou blanc **3.90**
CHAUSSETTES mercerisées, blanches ou champagne **1.30**
En albène mat, blanc, tricot serré . . . **2.15**
En laine unie, blanche **2.15**
BAS sport à revers, en marine, rouge, beige ou gris **2.70**

ÉLÉGANCE

SOLIDITÉ

Prix très

raisonnables

TOUT DOU... TOUT DOUCEMENT.   1 Couverture, 1 drap, 1 taie.

Opposite page: In addition to catalogs of Bleuette's extensive wardrobe items, Gautier-Languereau also published catalogs for the children's books they offered. This example from 1936 is die-cut and filled with selections telling the stories of Bécassine's many adventures.

Advertisements in La Semaine de Suzette *offered books, costumes, and even Bécassine dolls. This advertisement features a variety of footwear for Bleuette.*

A recipe for Hollandaise sauce was contributed by the evocatively named *Pétale de Rose thé* (Rose Petal Tea), with instructions as follows:

6 spoonfuls of powdered sugar, sifted
6 spoonfuls of water
6 spoonfuls of wine
6 well-beaten eggs
juice and peel of one lemon
To make: Mix all ingredients together; then bring to a boil. Pour to cool.

In addition to recipes, table-setting ideas were given, including lessons on folding napkins in fanciful shapes. Sometimes simple directions for making a centerpiece for the table were offered to the readers. Finally, lessons in table manners were not neglected. They ranged from "not eating and laughing at the same time" to guidance as to which implement to use for various kinds of food.

In studying Bleuette, understanding the complexity and depth of *La Semaine de Suzette* is important. The magazine, with its broad range of articles and activities, is worthy of its own separate study. The fine tradition of children's publications of high quality in France is a fascinating topic for further research. For this book, however, it is important to understand how essential Bleuette was to the launching of the magazine and to its enduring popularity. The modern collector finds it difficult to imagine Bleuette outside the context of the life instructions and patterns presented in *La Semaine de Suzette*. Imagining the magazine as an important part of French girlhood for fifty years without the presence of Bleuette is equally difficult.

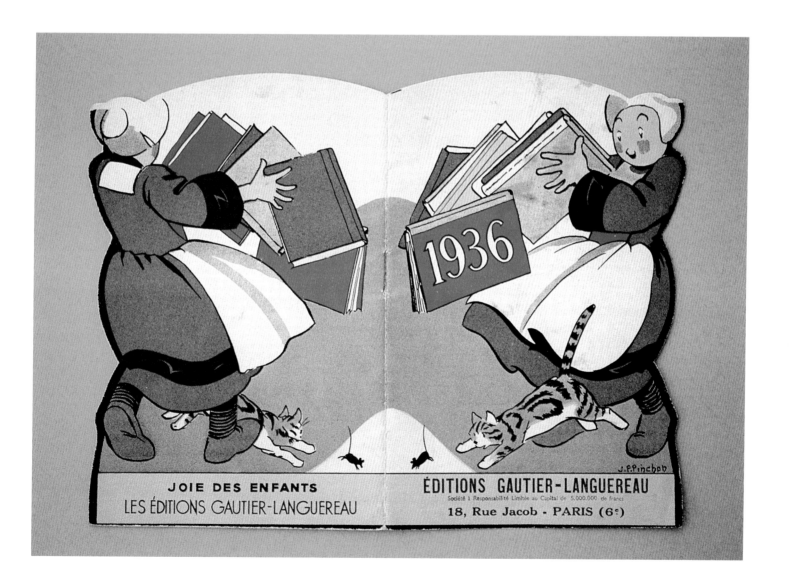

JOIE DES ENFANTS
LES ÉDITIONS GAUTIER-LANGUEREAU

ÉDITIONS GAUTIER-LANGUEREAU
Société à Responsabilité Limitée au Capital de 5.000.000 de francs
18, Rue Jacob - PARIS (6ᵉ)

4

WHO IS BLEUETTE?

In 1905, as goods and services became affordable for more people, society rapidly moved beyond the time when a family's necessities had to be produced in the home. The new, more leisurely lifestyle allowed children more time for the pursuit of play. Girls had always been encouraged to mimic such adult social behavior as tea parties, social calls, and even funerals in their play with dolls. Dolls also served the very practical purpose of teaching little girls the feminine arts, such as sewing, fine needlework and childcare, as well as a sense of fashion and style. Since the intent of the new magazine, *La Semaine de Suzette*, was to provide instruction in the skills and values that the little girls would need when they became the "future wives and mothers of France," what better teaching tool than a doll? With dolls at the height of popularity, what better way was there to encourage girls to subscribe to the new magazine?

As the publishers of *La Semaine de Suzette* sought a special doll to serve as premium and mascot for their new magazine, the world of French dollmaking was changing forever. In 1899, the fine manufacturers of French luxury dolls, considered all over the world as the ultimate in desirability and beauty, finally lost their battle for market share to the cheaper, more efficiently produced German-made dolls. In an effort to remain

*This Première Bleuette is
all set to go for a walk in the
garden in her vintage cotton dress
with tucking and flounce,
French antique leather boots,
and vintage straw hat.
The dress has a miniature
jacquard weave and a dainty
brown dot design.*

Collectors must be aware that SFBJ made dolls that were very similar in size to Bleuette, with heads marked very much like Bleuette's head. One example is this vividly colored SFBJ doll, marked "71 Unis France 149 301." She also has her original gold foil Jumeau tag and her original labeled Jumeau box. She is 28.5 centimeters tall. But she is not a Bleuette. The Jumeau-labeled dolls were never sold as Bleuette. Likewise, dolls similar to Bleuette, but marked "Au Nain Bleu," were made and sold only at the exclusive Paris toy shop of that name. Bleuettes were not sold by any store; they were available only through Gautier-Languereau.

viable, several French dollmakers joined together with two German dollmakers (Solomon Fleischmann and Bloëdel) who owned factories in France, to form the *Société Française de Fabrication de Bébés et Jouets.* The initials, SFBJ, were registered in 1905. It was to this new collaboration of dollmakers that Henri Gautier went to secure an exclusive contract to manufacture a doll for use as a premium for his new magazine, *La Semaine de Suzette.*

SFBJ offered the high standards associated with French dollmaking, combined with the reasonable cost and efficiency of German production. Solomon Fleischmann, a German by birth, who was married to a French woman, provided the early leadership for the company. He contributed about $200,000 to the SFBJ enterprise, and received one thousand shares of stock, second only to the holdings of Emile Jumeau. Fleischmann led the toymaking cooperative until pressures from World War I forced him to live in exile in Spain. Sadly, he had never taken time to formalize his relationship with his adopted country of France. Fleischmann died in Spain before the end of World War I.[18]

Although Bleuette was introduced towards the end of the glory days of French dollmaking, we can well imagine that the publishers of *La Semaine de Suzette* selected a Tête Jumeau mold for the Première (first) Bleuette to reflect the aura of privilege associated with the luxury dolls of France. By advertising the doll with the Jumeau name, Gautier was responding to nationalistic pride, and assuring his customers that the dolls would be of the finest quality and entirely French in origin.

However, the eager collector of Bleuette needs to be aware that SFBJ also produced 28-centimeter (11-inch) dolls, with heads marked like Bleuette's, sold under the trade name "Jumeau." Often these dolls were sold in a box marked "Jumeau," as well. Because of the difficulty in authenticating these dolls, Bleuette collectors usually avoid the 28-centimeter dolls. Also, although the French were extremely proud of their reputation as the world's finest dollmakers, many of the Jumeau heads were, in fact, made in Germany, then shipped to France for assemblage into dolls.

One way to discern immediately if a doll is a Bleuette is to look at her hands; the nails and joints on the fingers of the Jumeau dolls that are *not* Bleuettes are

painted with very fine red lines. The heads manufactured in Germany tend to have a ruddier complexion than the fine bisque of the heads made in France. The doll heads made in Germany also often have an additional mark, besides the 1 or 2 you might expect to find. An "X" or "Y" are characteristic marks on German-made heads on French dolls.

Difficulty in manufacturing dolls with consistent quality soon became an issue for SFBJ—and Bleuette. One result of dwindling revenue and streamlined manufacturing process seems to have been an attitude of expediency on the part of SFBJ. As a result, various molds were used for Bleuette, over time, as back stock was exhausted. The markings on the heads and bodies of Bleuette also lacked consistency. Even the size and form of the composition bodies changed with time. Thus, any survey of molds used to create Bleuette requires diligence and close study.

Because Henri Gautier conceived the idea of using a doll as a premium before he even published the first issue of *La Semaine de Suzette*, and sold out the first 20,000 Bleuettes before the first issue of the magazine was published, the need for expediency was established from the beginning of Bleuette's production. For much of Bleuette's history, demand far outstripped supply.

THE PREMIÈRE BLEUETTE

The first Bleuette has a pale, poured-porcelain head of fine quality. The painting is lush and beautifully refined. Often these first Bleuettes have very strong, multi-stroke eyebrows. The lips are painted with a rose-coral color that was fashionable in 1905. The most accepted mark on these dolls is the numeral "2" marked over an incised numeral "1," on the upper part of the neck. As with several of the Bleuette dolls, however, there is some confusion and disagreement on which marks were used for the Première Bleuette. In researching this issue, Hélène Bugat-Pujol found several references in the pages of *La Semaine de Suzette* that Bleuette was a "*Bébé Jumeau, size number 2.*"[19] This finding does not dispute the known facts: that the Première was 27 centimeters (10 5/8 inches) in height and made from a Jumeau mold. The question is: which Jumeau size was used for this first doll? In her writing, Hélène Bugat-Pujol cites two references to the doll's height from the pages of *La Semaine de Suzette*, found

During the fifty-five years of her production, Bleuette's face and even her body evolved and changed. A thorough study of the several faces of Bleuette is important to identifying which dolls are authentic Bleuette dolls—and which simply want to be. The first Bleuette doll was ordered by Henri Gautier from SFBJ. She was to have a porcelain head from a Jumeau head mold, fully jointed body of composition and wood, and she was to come dressed in a simple chemise. This lovely example of the 1905 Première Bleuette has the sought-after look of the Jumeau dolls with her heavily painted eyebrows, oily bisque, and precisely painted mouth. She is 27 centimeters in height and has four little teeth. She has threaded blue paperweight eyes. The wig is hand-wefted human hair, possibly from her first "mama's" own hair.

The Première Bleuette is much sought-after. She seems always to have a wondering look of innocence. This lucky doll is costumed in a dress made for her by Louise Hedrick, using the pattern for the "Robe d'Été" in issue 24 of La Semaine de Suzette, 1908.

in a regular feature called *"La Petite Poste"* (the little post office). The first reference is in issue number 37, 1905, when *Tante Jacqueline* wrote to a young reader that Bleuette is *"une Jumeau Taille 2,"* (Jumeau, size (height) 2). Again in issue number 49, 1906, she wrote that Bleuette was *"une poupée numero 2."*[20]

The Première Bleuette has inset glass eyes, usually blue, often paperweight, and an open mouth with four carved teeth. Her wig is made of long, wavy mohair or human hair. The composition body is fully jointed in the French manner, with carefully tapered sections on the arms, hands, legs and thighs where the wood or composition parts are joined. The torso is well-modeled, and the hips curve smoothly over the upper-thigh joining. (The German composition bodies use a system of wooden balls at the joints.)

This Bleuette is characterized by an acute angled cut on the back of the head through which the eyes were mounted in the head. The doll came dressed in a simple chemise (to encourage the new doll "mother" to begin sewing a wardrobe for her doll immediately). The fabric of the chemise was similar to our modern cheesecloth and was made into a straight, shift-style garment. The only decoration was a piece of lace stitched diagonally across the chemise, from the shoulder to just below the natural waist. Later versions had two rows of vertical lace and blue ribbon stitched to the front, from the shoulder to the hemline. Very few of these chemises are found today, as they were neither sturdy nor particularly attractive. These chemises were typical of those found on many French dolls of this era.

This first Bleuette is referred to as the Première Bleuette, not a "Jumeau-Bleuette." Although Henri Gautier was certainly counting on the fact that people would realize Bleuette was a doll of high quality because her head was made from a Jumeau mold, the name Jumeau does not appear on Bleuette or on the packing box in which she was sold. The last true dolls made by Emile Jumeau and his factory were created in 1899. To produce Bleuette in 1905, the SFBJ used a Jumeau mold they acquired when Emile Jumeau sold his inventory of molds to the new federation of French dollmakers.

Throughout the production of the doll, the height of a Bleuette is critical in making a definite identification

The first 20,000 Bleuettes ordered by Henri Gautier were distributed as premiums for La Semaine de Suzette, *before the first issue was even published. This wistful Première was displayed at the Musée de la Poupée during the Bleuette Exhibition in Paris in 2000. She is wearing a* broderie anglaise *dress made for her by Suzanne Gautrot of Paris, from the first pattern offered in* La Semaine de Suzette, *February 2, 1905.*

that a particular doll is, indeed, a true Bleuette. Bleuette was 27 centimeters (10 5/8 inches) tall until 1933, when she grew to 29 centimeters (11 3/8 inches). (A transitional period did occur in 1932, when both sizes were made.) As with most dolls, there are a few documented exceptions, but they are extremely rare, and collectors are advised to carry a tape measure and question any doll that deviates from the standard sizes.

The Première Bleuette is much sought-after today, just as she was when she was introduced in 1905. When found for sale today, this doll commands the very highest prices, from $3,200 to $9,000, depending on condition, clothing, and accessories—such as a trunk in good condition, hats, original shoes and stockings, etc.

At the same time as the French-made Première Bleuette was in production, similar doll heads were being manufactured in Germany through a special agreement, according to author Colette Merlen.[21] These non-Bleuette dolls were sold at the Trois-Quartiers, the

only store authorized by Gautier-Languereau to sell the Bleuette-type doll. Gautier-Languereau had the exclusive rights to 27-centimeter dolls made to the specifications of their Bleuette. The dolls sold at Trois-Quartiers had sleep eyes and cost more than Bleuette. These dolls were not sold as Bleuette. Gautier-Languereau was the only source for the purchase of a Bleuette. The modern collector must be aware that throughout the years of Bleuette's production similar dolls were sold that were not Bleuettes.

6/0 BLEUETTE

The second Bleuette was made using a German mold owned by Fleischmann and Blödel. Fleischmann was in charge when the second Bleuette dolls, marked 6/0, in an ornate style typical of old German script, were produced. The 6/0 Bleuette seems to have been an effort by SFBJ to meet the great demand for Bleuettes. Determining precise dating for her production as a Bleuette is difficult, but she appears to have been sold between 1905 and 1914. When

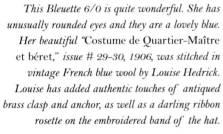

This Bleuette 6/0 is quite wonderful. She has unusually rounded eyes and they are a lovely blue. Her beautiful "Costume de Quartier-Maître et béret," issue # 29-30, 1906, was stitched in vintage French blue wool by Louise Hedrick. Louise has added authentic touches of antiqued brass clasp and anchor, as well as a darling ribbon rosette on the embroidered band of the hat.

This Bleuette 6/0 is wearing a navy-blue velvet dress with deep blue leather trim at the neck, sleeve and dress hem. Her vintage hand-made hat is lined in silk jacquard. A leather belt with brass buckles completes this ensemble, based on "Trottinette," from the Spring 1928 Gautier-Languereau catalog.

*This winsome 6/0 is wearing a costume that is
a tremendous favorite among Bleuette "mothers."
The pattern was offered in issue #30, 1911,
in* La Semaine de Suzette. *The dress is called
simply "Robe." The dark accents against the golden
silk taffeta are all hand-embroidered. The
small black fan in front of the doll is also handmade.*

SFBJ began producing the third version of the Bleuette
dolls, the little 6/0 was retired.

The head of the 6/0 is usually made of bisque of fine
quality, and is marked only with the numbers 6/0 at the
nape of the neck in the same ornate German-style
numerals. Sometimes there is an additional small figure
incised above the 6/0, which may be the mark of the
individual who painted the particular head. It is not
always present. This doll has four teeth in her open
mouth, just like the Première Bleuette.

The doll is always 27 centimeters tall on a fully jointed
body. The bodies are sometimes marked with a number
2 between the shoulder blades.

Although not considered as pretty as the Première
Bleuette, the little 6/0 has a particularly loyal group of
collectors. They are drawn to her winsome little face
with its small, dark eyes and wistful expression. Prices
for 6/0 Bleuettes have risen steadily in recent years,
from the $700 range to well over $1,000 in 2001.

At the same time as the 6/0 head mold was used for
Bleuette, there was a similar head mold used for a doll
that is *not* a Bleuette.[22] The non-Bleuette doll that is
marked "SFBJ 60 PARIS 6/0" is one of a series of SFBJ
dolls made in various sizes, (*i.e.* 4/0, 6/0, 8/0). The doll
with the SFBJ 60 6/0 head has a somewhat larger head
circumference than the true Bleuette. To the unwary,
this non-Bleuette may be mistaken for a 6/0 or for the
SFBJ 60 8/0, which was produced immediately after the
6/0.[23] Only a 27-centimeter doll marked 6/0 is a
Bleuette. A 27-centimeter doll marked 8/0 was not sold
as a Bleuette. (After 1915, however, the SFBJ 60 8/0
was sold as Bleuette.) The SFBJ 60 must be incised
above the 8/0 for the doll to be a Bleuette.

The 6/0 mold was used from 1905 through 1914.
Although the firm of Gautier-Languereau always had
a solid reputation as a French firm, when they con-
tracted with SFBJ to make the heads for their mascot
doll, Bleuette, they opened the door to German-made
heads being imported for this very French little girl,
Bleuette. For economic reasons, Fleischmann shipped
the Jumeau head molds to Germany for production of
some of those heads, as well. The finished heads were
shipped back to France for assemblage with the bodies. The heads Fleischmann imported from Germany

were used until the SFBJ mold 60, size 8/0 replaced the earlier 6/0 mold.

Prior to 1914, Bleuettes were made from the palest fine bisque. Many had pierced ears, a beguiling dimple on the chin, and lips carefully painted a warm-red color. However, as on many dolls manufactured by SFBJ, neither the quality of the bisque nor of the painting was consistently good.

SFBJ 60 PARIS, 8/0 BLEUETTE

In 1915, the Fleischmann mold was replaced with SFBJ mold 60, size 8/0. After 1924, the signature 71 Unis France 149 was sometimes used instead of the SFBJ signature, but the numbers 60 8/0 were used in both cases.

Next in the long line of Bleuette dolls is the SFBJ 60 8/0, also sometimes marked "71 Unis France 149 8/0." This little cello player, in her original wig, is wearing a dress from 1913 called "Aele" and shoes sold by Gautier-Languereau. The costume was also created as a pattern in 1914 in La Semaine de Suzette, *issue 25. The pattern is called "Petite Robe de Plage."*

When the original order for Bleuette dolls was disbursed so quickly, another order was placed by Gautier for more dolls. SFBJ filled this second order by using, in part, a Fleischmann & Blöedel head mold, marked simply 6/0. This wistful child is wearing a charming dress made by Hélène Bugat-Pujol of Paris, from the pattern for a Robe Habillée, *issue #4, 1915.*

A favorite early pattern in La Semaine de Suzette *is this "Casino" dress from 1906, issues 25-26. Louise Hedrick stitched this dress using antique fabrics and silk ribbons in 2001. The Bleuette is marked "SFBJ 60 8/0."*

Bleuette, like many other antique dolls, has an enigma. This doll is the correct size for a Bleuette, 27 centimeters. She came in a trunk with a wardrobe of Gautier-Languereau costumes. She certainly looks like a 60 8/0. However, there is absolutely no mark on her head. Is this the exception that proves the rule? How did one head manage to proceed through a factory with no mark? Her face was painted by skilled hands. She wears a simple silk chemise.

Another signature sometimes used at that time was SFBJ 301 1. These dolls were all 27 centimeters tall. The signature "block" was in the center of the back of the dolls head. Remember, though, that the Unis France signature was used only after 1924.[24] Sometimes, the last two digits of the year of manufacture are also incised into the back of the head; *i.e.* "22" or "24." These additional numerals, however, were not used consistently.

After 1919, some of the Bleuettes were made with sleep eyes. But by 1922, all Bleuettes were offered with sleep eyes. The height of the dolls remained 27 centimeters until 1932. Many collectors consider the period covering 1920 to the late 1930s as the "golden age" of Bleuette. The fine quality of the dolls remained consistent, and the clothing offered by Gautier-Languereau was diverse and beautifully crafted by fine seamstresses.

Beginning in 1922, Bleuettes were manufactured with composition as well as with poured-bisque heads. Just as two different molds were used simultaneously, so were the two different head materials. The Bleuettes with composition heads may measure slightly larger

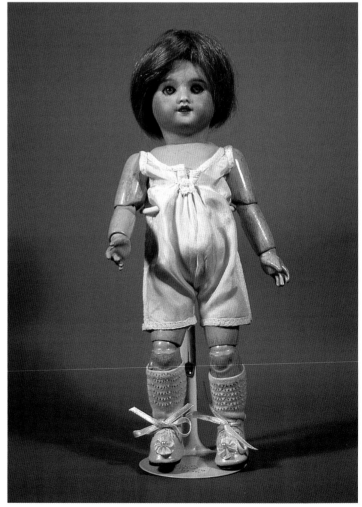

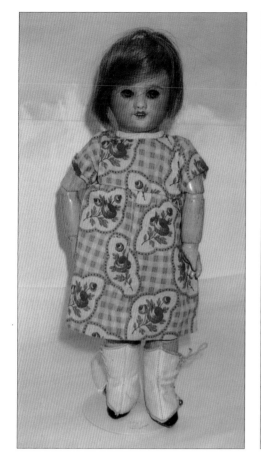

Above, far left: Complementing this SFBJ 60 8/0 is her bright dress, "Blanchette et Rose," from the Gautier-Languereau catalog of Summer 1923.

Above left: This SFBJ 60 8/0 is wearing her original chemise. These garments were made of very inexpensive, thin, woven fabric that looks something like our cheesecloth. Unfortunately, many of the original chemises were thrown out when they collapsed from washing, or because they were thought to be unimportant.

Above: Made between 1929 and 1931, this Bleuette 60 8/0 is sometimes called a "transitional" Bleuette. She is 27 centimeters tall and is marked with a 2 on her back and a 1 on each foot. She has a replaced, human-hair wig. She is wearing a charming smocked dress that was very popular from 1936 to 1940, appearing in every Gautier-Languereau catalog during those years.

than their bisque-headed sisters; composition does not shrink as porcelain does in firing.

The Bleuettes with heads marked 60, with 8/0 on the nape of the neck, are characterized by very round cheeks, a smooth chin, slender eyebrows and finely painted lashes. The open mouths are deep red, with four little teeth showing. The bisque is generally of nice quality, but the painting at times is rather imprecise. The lips may be painted a bit crooked and the eyebrows may show very casual placement. The eye-cuts also vary, from doll to doll, and even on individual dolls, with one eye cut markedly larger than the other. For their avid collectors, all this variation simply adds to the charm of these little dolls.

SFBJ AND UNIS FRANCE 301 BLEUETTE

The designation "Unis France" does not indicate the name of a company or a manufacturer. Rather, the words assure the purchaser that all parts of an object marked with these words have been made in France. The letters stand for *Union Nationale Inter-Syndicale* (or, National Union of Trade Syndicates). This union was formed in 1915 and promoted French-made products. There are three numbers associated with the Unis

In 1933, without explanation, Bleuette suddenly grew two centimeters in height. At the same time, her torso slimmed down and her legs and arms became longer and more slender. This new model Bleuette had an SFBJ or Unis France 301 head. These dolls are more frequently seen since they were among the most recently made. This trio of Unis France 301 Bleuettes show some of the variation in the faces. The doll on the left, wearing her original wig, has lovely oily bisque and simple, one-stroke eyebrows. She wears a homemade dress and vest in vintage fabric. The doll in the center has a replaced wig and a very soft expression. Her silk dress is made in vintage tissue silk from a pattern in La Semaine de Suzette, *issue 19, 1922. These dolls were produced in the early 1950s. The Bleuette on the right wears her original wig. She was made just after World War II, when supplies for dollmaking were of poor quality, and in short supply. The cheek blush and detail painting of eyelashes and eyebrows has disappeared. This was caused by unstable paint mixtures at that time. She wears a vintage dress made from rows of silk ribbon stitched together to form a colorful fabric.*

France mark. The numeral to the left of the words indicates which trade union made the object. The numeral to the right was a special number given to members by the trade union to which they belonged. The central number, *i.e.* 60 or 301, indicates the mold number of the head, in the case of dolls.[25]

The first dolls with heads from the 301 mold were 27 centimeters tall. Sometimes, these dolls are considered transitional, since they were introduced in the 27 centimeter-size, but soon "grew" to 29 centimeters (11 3/8 inches). Some of the early 301 heads, marked either "SFBJ PARIS," or "71 UNIS FRANCE 149," have an additional mark: "1."

Although there was no special announcement, Bleuette grew two centimeters in 1933. The new size was reflected in the patterns, which were adjusted to fit the taller doll. The height was achieved by lengthening the upper thigh by one centimeter, and slightly enlarging the head. These changes gave Bleuette a slightly more mature appearance. She remained 29 centimeters high, until the late 1950s when a new plastic model was introduced. The 29-centimeter size was noted by the addition of the numerals "1-1/4" on the back of the porcelain-headed doll's neck, on porcelain heads, and the numerals "1-1/2" on the composition-headed dolls. The heads marked "UNIS FRANCE" bear the additional marks of 71 and 149. The heads marked "SFBJ PARIS 301" may also have two digits denoting the year of manufacture, *i.e.* "22" or "24," and may have the figure "1" carved in the nape of the neck. These first 301 Bleuettes, made before 1933, were 27 centimeters high.

The 301 head mold has a charm all its own. Because this head was used throughout the years leading up to World War II, and after the war, there is great variation in the quality of the bisque and the painting. The dolls produced in the years after the war often have very little paint tint of any kind on the cheeks. During that period of time, the paint used on the dolls was unstable due to poor ingredients and readily washed, or wiped off, the porcelain. On the opposite end of the spectrum, many 301 Bleuettes produced in the late 1940s and early 1950s are very ruddy-colored bisque, with flaming red cheeks and bright red lips. The eyebrows are painted with multi-strokes, but remain fairly narrow.

The 301 remains a favorite of collectors today. She has a saucy appearance and seems ready to head into any new

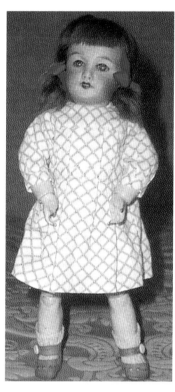

Far left: This Unis France 301 is wearing a Gautier-Languereau dress named "Heureuse," from the Summer 1932 catalog. The doll was offered at auction in Chartres, France recently.

Left: Perhaps one of the most appealing features of the 301s is their bright attitude. These dolls just seem to say that they are ready for an adventure. As all SFBJ and Unis France 301 dolls, this Bleuette is the correct 29 centimeters and has lovely blue sleep eyes.

Top: One final look at a Bleuette 301, looking very saucy in her blue crocheted hat and dress by Gautier-Languereau, The doll is marked "71 Unis France 149 301 1-1/4." She has a "2" on her back and a "1" on each foot. She is wearing a "Robe Standard" from the late 1940s.

Above: This Bleuette has a well-preserved label on her back. The original paper stamp states: "Bleuette Modèle Déposé."

adventure proposed by her "mother." The 29-centimeter doll, despite having a rather generic, cylindrical form to the upper arms and thighs, was able to wear the many costumes in Bleuette's trousseau with grace and style. The look of eager anticipation in her sweet face continues to capture the hearts of Bleuette collectors today.

The most common mold numbers found are the SFBJ 60 and 301, later marked "UNIS FRANCE 301." It is important for the collector to remember that all dolls marked "SFBJ 60" did not come from the same mold.[26] This fact, coupled with the variation in the quality of painting, may account for some of the confusion for collectors seeking authentic Bleuettes. It is also wise to remember that at the time SFBJ was using up the stock of molds of several doll companies. Thus a head marked SFBJ can be found on a variety of bodies, not necessarily of French manufacture. In addition, after the formation of the SFBJ cooperative, the French purchased much cheaper German-made heads, put them on Jumeau bodies, and sold them in boxes marked Jumeau. Bleuette, however, was not sold in a Jumeau-marked box. She was sold in a simple, corrugated cardboard box, packed with tissue.

The difference in price between dolls of French manufacture and those produced in Germany or Great Britain occurred in large part because the French used highly-skilled adult labor. These workers had to be paid considerably more than the unskilled workforce in Germany and Britain.[27]

GÉGÉ

In the years 1958-1960, the final doll in the Bleuette family was produced. She is called Bleuette 58, or Gégé. She is made of plastic with a five-piece jointed body. She measures 33 centimeters (13 inches) tall, and is marked "Gégé" on the back of her head. Her body is marked: "Made in France, Gégé, 8A, Déposé." She has a closed mouth with bright red lips. Her sleep eyes are blue and she has blonde comb-able hair. One can surmise that Gautier-Languereau felt a need to modernize Bleuette, and thus proposed this new doll. This Bleuette

The final doll sold by Gautier-Languereau was a 33-centimeter plastic or rheubroid doll named Gégé. Her head is marked with her name, and her body has an 8-A mark. She is sometimes referred to as Bleuette 58.

Gégé has a simplified body and truly bears little resemblance to Bleuette. A few ensembles were offered in the Gautier-Languereau catalogs of the late 1950s for this doll.

Below and opposite page: Bleuette 58, who was also called Gégé, was advertised in La Semaine de Suzette *and the Gautier-Languereau catalogs, of 1959-1960, at the very end of Bleuette's production. A few costumes were also offered in her new size of 33 centimeters (13 inches).*

58 is very difficult to find. Like Rosette, Gégé was not exclusively made for Gautier-Languereau, which compounds the problem for people who wish to collect her. BillyBoy suggests she may have been made using the Careen mold owned by the Gégé Company.[28]

While very modern in appearance, Gégé has a certain charm that recalls her older-sister Bleuettes. Although she was introduced at the very end of the publication of *La Semaine de Suzette*, there were several patterns published for her in 1959 and 1960. The last catalogs also listed clothing for La Grande Bleuette 58.

ATYPICAL BLEUETTES

One of the challenging aspects of studying Bleuette is that for every hard-and-fast-rule, there seems to be an exception. We are steadily gaining new knowledge and insight into this doll that has so captured the imaginations of doll lovers for nearly a century. Most of the

Above right: Although Bleuette was "born" in Paris, she has found wide acceptance all over the world. This beautiful Unis France 301, holding her celluloid Petitcolin, is a favorite of her owner in Japan.

Right: This sweet Bleuette is marked 60 8/0 and is 27 centimeters tall. Her body is marked "2" and there is a "1" on both feet. Her wig is replaced. Her owner was told only the head is truly a Bleuette's.

Bleuette
Rosette et
Bambino

HIVER 1959-1960

GAUTIER-LANGUEREAU — 18, rue Jacob - Paris-6e   DAN. 35-44

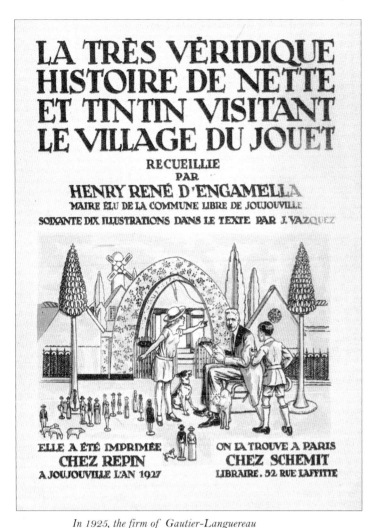

In 1925, the firm of Gautier-Languereau participated in a display of toys and dolls at the Joujouville portion of the Exhibition of the Decorative Arts in Paris. In 1927, the celebrated German author Henry d'Allemagne wrote a book entitled La Trés Veridique Histoire de Nette et Tintin Visitant le Village du Jouet (*The Very True Story of Nette and Tintin Visiting the Toy Village), about this exhibition under his pseudonym: Henry-Rene d'Engamella. One of the illustrations in this book showed a number of Bleuettes, including an SFBJ 251 doll wearing a Bécassine costume, supporting the later contention that an SFBJ 251 was indeed sold as Bleuette. Above is the frontispiece of d'Allemagne's book.*

exceptions are truly rare, but they do exist. The collector must be as aware of the exceptions as of those dolls that fit the rules. Several exceptions have already been noted. In addition, the following are worth noting:

According to BillyBoy, author of *Bleuette: La petite fille modèle de la collection*, the daughter of Claude Languereau has confirmed that in rare instances, when supplies of the wooden thighs for the 27-centimeter Bleuette ran short, a thigh intended for a larger doll was occasionally substituted, resulting in a doll that measured 28 centimeters high. Gautier-Languereau also sold dolls with heads that were marked with the SFBJ or Unis France signature, mold #301, with the additional incised name of Jumeau, in boxes with labels marked Jumeau. In spite of the markings on the head, these Jumeau dolls were not Bleuettes.[29]

While the usual marking on Bleuette's feet is the numeral "1" incised in the sole of each foot, the collector should be aware that some of the early dolls with the 6/0 heads made in Germany may have been marked so faintly that the mark virtually disappeared during the painting process.[30] The numeral "2" between the shoulder blades, which is usually found on Bleuette's torso, is occasionally obscured by a faint mark and heavy painting. Also, a doll as popular as Bleuette would most likely have been taken for repairs if it became damaged. Since these dolls belonged to children and were avidly played with over many years, it is reasonable to assume that some Bleuettes today are on replaced bodies.

In at least one instance, a lovely Bleuette has been found with her Gautier-Languereau wardrobe, but absolutely no identifying marks on the back of her head. After careful study of the doll, French doll authorities determined this doll is, indeed, a Bleuette. This conclusion was reached because the doll, her trunk and her original Gautier-Langeuereau wardrobe had been in the family since it was originally purchased. The doll measured 27 centimeters and looked just like a Bleuette. With the addition of a confirmed provenance from the original owners, her authenticity was established.

SFBJ 251

When Bleuette collectors are together, there is often lively discussion about the chubby-faced SFBJ 251, size 2 doll. This doll, with a younger toddler-type face, has been a favorite of doll collectors for many years. The only ques-

This composition Unis France 301 is comfortable wearing "Double Emploi" from the Summer 1950 catalog. Bleuette is accompanied by "Ric," the dog designed by Gautier-Languereau.

This perky SFBJ 251 is wearing a completely original Scotish plaid ensemble called "Bon Petit Diable" in the Winter 1934–45 Gautier-Languereau catalog. Note the well-painted face and oily bisque in this fine example.

tion is whether this little doll was ever sold as a Bleuette. Perhaps the most persuasive evidence that she may have been is contained in a book by Henry d'Allemagne, a German who wrote books about toys in the early 1900s. In 1927, using the pseudonym Henry-Rene d'Engamella, he published *La Trés Véridique Histoire de Nette et Tintin Visitant le Village du Jouet* (The Very True Story of Nette and Tintin Visiting the Toy Village). This book followed the 1925 *Exposition Internationale des Arts Décoratifs et Industriels Modernes* (Exhibition of Ornamental Arts), which featured French-made toys in the *Joujouville* (Village of Toys). The Exposition was conceived as a way to promote the French toymaking industry.

The Exposition was set up in an actual little village of wooden house fronts surrounding a mill; all were gaily painted and crafted by French artisans. Each house contained the display of a noted French toy manufacturer. The firm of Gautier-Languereau sponsored two of the booths. Children were invited to attend the Exposition, where they could walk into a make-believe village filled with their favorite toys and dolls. They were urged to go

A budding beautician seems to have been at work on this little 251. Note the wig all tied up with rags to form pretty curls for some special occasion. This SFBJ 251 came to her present owner as you see her— and probably just as her former "mama" left her. The doll is dressed in a robe, nightie and socks sold by Gautier-Languereau. The slippers were made from a pattern in La Semaine de Suzette.

and see Bleuette and her latest summer clothing.

An illustration by J. Vazquez from the book shows this artist's rendition of one of the toy houses, which was set in a village motif. In a large, curtained window, a photograph of the display of a number of Bleuettes is shown framed by the artist-drawn house of Gautier-Languereau. At the far left-hand front corner in the photograph is an SFBJ 251 doll wearing a Bécassine costume.

Bleuette researchers had long suspected that the SFBJ 251 head mold was used as a Bleuette head on some dolls. But there appeared to be no proof of this. In 1992, Colette Merlen wrote in her book, *Bleuette: Poupée de la Semaine de Suzette*, that it was her "inmost conviction" that the SFBJ 251 was a Bleuette. Elisabeth Chauveau agreed in the second volume of *Nous Habillons Bleuette, 1923-1933*, published in 1998. Both authors suggested that the #251 Bleuette was possibly descended from Benjamine. However, the photograph from the Toy Village in 1925 clearly shows a #251 dressed as Bécassine. Benjamine was not introduced until 1926. This image of an SFBJ 251 amongst the Bleuettes seems to support the conclusion that Merlen and Chauveau made: that an SFBJ 251 was, indeed, sold as Bleuette.[31]

Antique doll dealers in France who specialize in Bleuette have mentioned repeatedly that the SFBJ 251 sold by Gautier-Languereau was most often found dressed as Bécassine. We can surmise that the company may have wanted to use a different head mold for the dolls they planned to sell dressed as Bécassine.

The SFBJ 251 has a head made of porcelain, composition or papier-mache. The head is marked "SFBJ" or "Unis France 251," size 2. She may be approximately 27 or 29 centimeters high. There is some variation in her height, depending upon the material of the head, and which body size is used. Her body and lower legs are made of composition. The arms and thighs are wooden. Her body is fully jointed, like Bleuette's. When a doll with a 251 head on a Bleuette-style body is found, she is frequently wearing clothing either made by Gautier-Languereau or from patterns in *La Semaine de Suzette.*

The doll with the 251 head on a baby body, like Benjamine, was not a commercial success. She lasted just a brief six months on the market. The 251 head on the Bleuette-type body, with a longer wig, appears to have been sold before, during, and after the production

of Benjamine. Perhaps the firm of Gautier-Languereau had a back stock of 251 heads when they pulled Benjamine from the market. The decision to place that head on a Bleuette body may have been primarily a business decision to use up heads that had already been produced. Shortly after the failure of Benjamine, the firm would bring out Bleuette's baby brother, using the same baby body used for Benjamine, but with the currently popular "natural-newborn" type head—softly painted, simply molded hair. This baby was far more successful for the firm than Benjamine.

Further research is necessary to unravel completely the mystery of the SFBJ 251 head doll. We do know that this doll was not exclusively produced for the firm of Gautier-Languereau. But when produced in the same size as Bleuette, she is frequently found with wonderful clothing either made, or inspired, by Gautier-Languereau. The 251, with her sweet toddler face, has many fans among Bleuette collectors today.

REPRODUCTION DOLLS

For the purists among Bleuette collectors, there is no substitute for the real Bleuettes. However, for the many collectors who cannot find or afford an original Bleuette, the reproductions offer a means of becoming a part of the enchanting circle of Bleuette's friends. Also, collectors who enjoy sewing wardrobes for their dolls often hesitate to put their antique dolls through the rigorous fitting process. The reproduction dolls offer an obvious solution to the need for a sturdy, "surrogate" Bleuette.

Today several excellent dollmakers are producing reproduction dolls of nice quality, with porcelain heads mounted on correct French composition bodies. These dolls are carefully marked on the inside of the bisque head, as well as on the outside, near the nape of the neck, with the dollmaker's mark and year of production. Ethical dollmakers always go to great lengths to be certain their work cannot be passed off as an original doll. These reproduction dolls are made with either sleep or inset eyes, and wigs of various colors and fibers. The reproductions fill a real need for people who wish to have a doll for which they can create a wardrobe of charming costumes from the patterns in *La Semaine de Suzette*.

Collectors need to be ever mindful that reproductions do exist. Occasionally, an unwary dealer receives a reproduction to sell, mistakenly labeled as a Bleuette.

This charming little doll is cute as can be—but she is not a Bleuette. She may well be a reproduction, which is why she has been included here. Remember, authentic marks appear on dolls that are not Bleuettes.

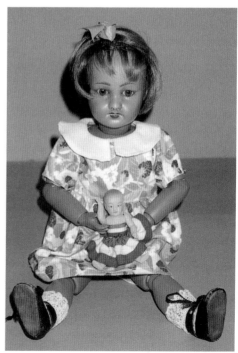

This 301 reproduction is a sweet little girl with Creole coloring, named Clonie. She also has inset glass or sleep eyes and a human-hair wig. She is wearing a simple cotton dress made in France. She holds her little celluloid Petitcolin doll, which is dressed in the colors of the French flag.

Even a cursory examination should tell the collector that the doll is of recent manufacture. The paint on the bodies looks very fresh and new, with a high gloss finish. Very few authentic Bleuettes have survived with their bodies in pristine condition. A close examination of the head reveals the marks incised on the inside and the fired-on signature mark of the reproduction artist on the outside. Obviously, a recently made head appears very white and clean on the inside bisque of the head. The plaster and eye mechanism are also sturdy, clean, and new. The reproduction French bodies are not marked on the torso or on the feet.

BLEUETTE'S BODY VARIATIONS

Not only did Bleuette's head change over time, her body did, as well. Originally, Bleuette was made with a Jumeau-type body. Obviously, for a child to be able to dress and undress the doll easily, the body needed to be fully articulated, including the wrists. Sadly, the nicely formed little hands and fingers are Bleuette's weakest point, throughout her production. The collector often finds Bleuettes whose bodies are in good condition—

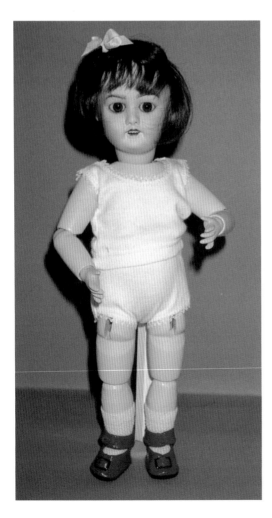

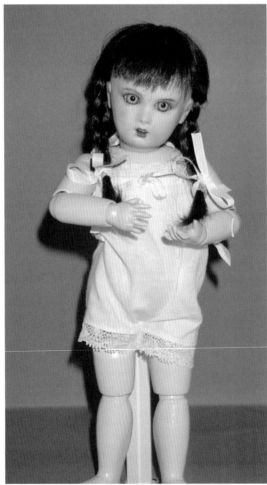

Above, far left: this French reproduction Unis France 301 with sleep eyes wears a human-hair wig and simple cotton knit underwear. She is 29 centimeters tall.

Above left: this Unis France reproduction has braids and deep-brown eyes. She is also 29 centimeters tall.

Far left: this perky little French reproduction of the SFBJ 60 8/0 doll has large round blue eyes and is 27 centimeters tall. Note the short, sturdy upper legs, compared to the longer, more cylindrical legs in the two examples above her.

Left: This sweet-faced doll was made as a favor for the first luncheon honoring Bleuette at the National Convention of the United Federation of Doll Clubs (UFDC) in New Orleans in 1998. The doll, made by June Hays and Barbara Hilliker, has a porcelain head made from a commercial Tete Jumeau mold and a jointed body.

Right: Just as Bleuette's face changed over time, so did her body. The Première Bleuette has a very compact, French body. The body is jointed at the neck, shoulders, elbows, wrists, hips, and knees. This pattern of jointing was used for all Bleuettes, until the end of production when plastic models were introduced. Her tummy shows a distinct belly-button.

Far right: In profile, we can see the steeply angled head cut that is typical of a Jumeau doll. This doll has a rather flat cork pate. The body is very nicely proportioned, compact, and suggests the doll could almost stand alone.

Below: A second Première Bleuette shows the distinctive, steep head cut.

Below right: Characteristics to look for in a Première Bleuette include: the high forehead and steep back-of-the-head-cut; heavy multi-stroke eyebrows; finely painted numerous eyelashes; large almond-shaped eyes; accent marks in the nostrils; an open mouth with four teeth showing; and lovely well-painted bisque. The doll may have pierced ears, or not.

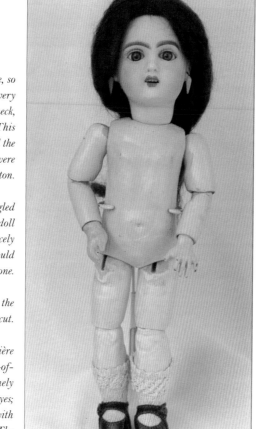

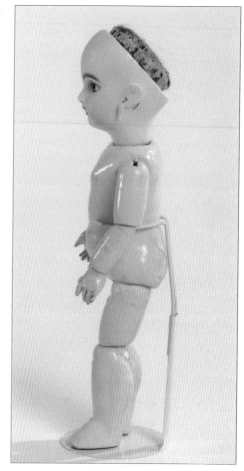

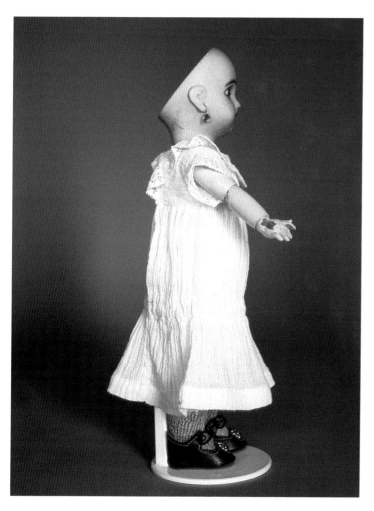

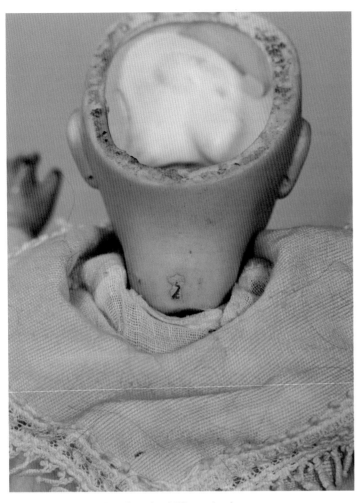

In any discussion of marks on Bleuette heads, there are always various opinions as to what is used on an authentic Bleuette. In the case of the Première, the most accepted mark is the number 1 superimposed with a numeral 2. As shown above, the number 1 is engraved into the bisque and a red numeral 2 is written on top of it. Jumeau heads marked with a simple 1 or 2 are often accepted as Bleuettes, if the height is exactly 27 centimeters. These bodies are unmarked.

except for missing fingers on one or both hands. Fingers on antique dolls almost always show some wear, as do the lower arms and legs. Fingers also suffer paint rubs as clothes are taken on and off the doll, or as they rub against protective wrapping while they are traveling. The earlier Bleuettes have beautiful, well-proportioned bodies, including the arms, legs and hands. Later in the production, the upper legs were over-simplified, and smaller, ill-proportioned hands were used.

The Bleuette bodies were nicely made of a composition material, rather than of the pressed and stapled cardboard used for less-expensive dolls of the era. The bodies are marked with the number "2" between the shoulder blades, and a "1" on the sole of each foot. The Première dolls, however, may have marks so faint they can barely be discerned. The early dolls have very round, protruding tummies and well-shaped hips. The belly button is represented by a small "dent" in the abdomen. Where the thighs connect to the torso of the body, the earlier dolls have a fairly realistic, smooth line from the leg up to the hip. In later dolls, the hips extend beyond the thigh on either side of the torso. The slots for stringing the legs show clearly in the front at the top of the thighs, and behind the knees on the lower legs. The knees are clearly molded into the lower leg. The lower legs are rather stocky and heavy looking.

Far left: In 1933, Bleuette's body was completely redesigned to give her a slimmer, older girl look. The torso was slightly elongated and stylized. The upper arms and thighs were simplified and elongated. The knee was barely suggested by a slight "dent" at the top of the lower leg. After 1933, all Bleuettes were 29 centimeters tall and had sleep eyes.

Left: Marked "71 Unis France 149 301," this doll has the typically elongated body of the later dolls. But this young lady is somewhat curvaceous compared to the doll at far left. This doll truly suggests the body of a preteen girl.

Sometimes, seeing faces side by side helps "fix" in the mind the subtle differences between various head molds. From left, we begin with the most recent, a 71 Unis France 149 301 with a 1-1/4 on the neck, 29 centimeters tall. She has the elongated, rather slender body of the later dolls, blue sleep eyes and her original wig. She was produced shortly after World War II. In the center is a perky little SFBJ 60 8/0. She is just 27 centimeters tall, with set blue eyes. She has her original wig and is dressed in a costume made by "mama" of checked silk taffeta. On the right is the earliest doll in this charming trio. She is marked simply 6/0 and was produced by SFBJ for Gautier between 1905 and 1914. She has deep-blue set eyes and a long blonde human-hair wig that may be original. Her costume was made by Suzanne Gautrot of Paris. Note the multi-stroke, heavy eyebrows on the 6/0 as compared to the single-stroke eyebrows of the later dolls. Also, in comparing the legs on the dolls, you can see that the earlier two dolls have much heavier lower legs than those of the 301. When studying Bleuettes from different decades, begin by examining how they are similar, then note the differences. Soon, you will find your eye is trained to quickly access and recognize the key characteristics of these interesting dolls.

In order to demonstrate the variations found in Bleuette bodies, the dolls posed for a group portrait. From left: SFBJ 60 8/0, Unis France 301 1, 6/0, Unis France 301 1-1/4, and a second Unis France 301 1-1/4. The first three dolls are 27 centimeters tall; the two on the right are 29 centimeters.

The joints are well made and allow ease of movement for the doll's arms, hands, legs and knees. The 27-centimeter Bleuettes are particularly well proportioned and balanced. They look amazingly life-like when posed in natural positions of play, which must have enchanted the little French doll mothers as much as it does collectors today.

When Bleuette grew to 29 centimeters in 1933, her body also changed. Her thighs and upper arms became longer and simplistic in appearance. Her torso was slimmer, suggesting the body of an older child. The head was enlarged slightly. Her lower legs were no longer as stocky as those of the earlier dolls.

Sometime in 1936, an article was published that continues to be cited, even though we have since learned that the information in it is wrong. The article stated that Bleuette's body was stapled together. While stapling was a common practice in the manufacture of less-expensive dolls, this method was not used in the

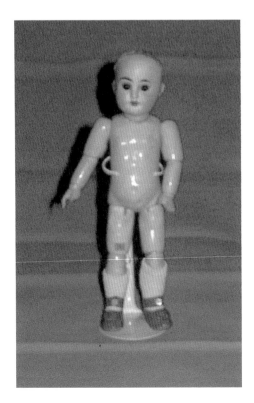

Far left: The 6/0, which was made concurrently with the Première Bleuette, has a very similar body. Legs, arms and torso are in excellent proportion which allows the doll to assume very natural, child-like poses. Note that the tummy protrudes. The head cut is much less steep than that on the Première's head.

Left: When examining doll bodies, especially Bleuette bodies, one quickly realizes that they came in many different flesh tones and had variations in one part of their anatomy or another. This "golden girl" has upper thighs that are of interest. She is marked "71 Unis France 149 60 8/0." Note the exaggerated cut on the front of the upper thigh. This was probably yet another effort to make the positioning of the doll more natural.

production of Bleuette. Her body was made by gluing the two halves of the body together, then carefully sanding the resulting seam lines until they were smooth, after which several coats of paint were added. The final step was a coating of varnish that provided a matte finish.[32]

The collector must remember that although the name Bleuette was reserved exclusively for use by the Gautier-Languereau publishing firm, very similar dolls were produced and sold at the same time in Paris. Well-known department stores such as Printemps and Galeries Lafayette sold dolls that were frank copies of Bleuette. These dolls were often sold in trunks with a wardrobe. Costumes in the wardrobe had similar names and styles to those currently in vogue for Bleuette. The outfits were less expensive, and were often chosen by parents for reasons of price. BillyBoy points out that SFBJ produced all the Bleuettes and the dolls of the same size sold by other

In profile, the varying degrees the tummies protrude is very clear. From left: SFBJ 60 8/0, 27 centimeters; Unis France 301 1-1/4, 29 centimeters; 6/0, 27 centimeters; Unis France 301 1, 27 centimeters; and Unis France 301, 29 centimeters.

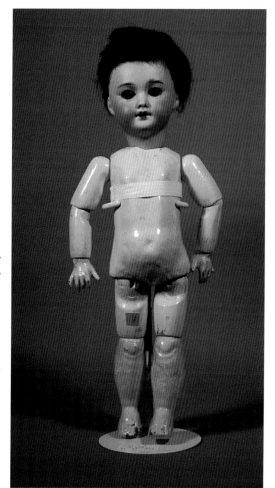

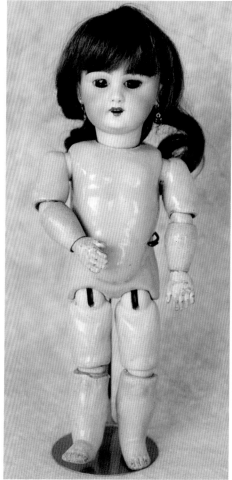

Right: This Bleuette, marked "22 SFBJ 301 Paris," clearly shows how compact and balanced the 27-centimeter dolls are. A stylized crescent in front of the joint suggests the knee.

Far right: For comparison purposes, this sweet-faced doll is NOT a Bleuette, but she is the correct size. She is of French manufacture, simply marked DEP. Her picture is included for comparison between the contemporary body of a non-Bleuette with the authentic Bleuettes. Compared to Bleuette's this body is somewhat out of proportion to the head. The elbow and knee joints are created by use of wooden ball-type joints. A pleasing little doll, but not a Bleuette.

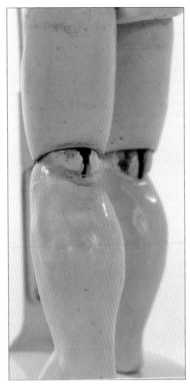

Left: A view from the back of the Première Bleuette shows the slotting that aids in stringing the lower leg to the thigh and allows for somewhat natural positioning of the doll. A similar slotting is seen at the connection of the upper arm to the shoulder.

Above: The back of the knees also has a distinctive, steeply angled cut to allow for maximum flexation of the knee. The lower leg is formed with a "knob" at the top which is designed to fit up into the lower end of the thigh. In well-made Jumeau-type bodies, this creates a very natural looking knee from the front view.

stores. The Bleuette heads produced after 1933 were marked with a 1-1/4 on the neck, but a doll of the same size that was just a copy would have a "1" or other number on her neck.[33]

Bleuette's hands were not painted with red lines highlighting the nails or finger creases. The hands were simply painted in a flesh tone.

Our job as Bleuette collectors would be much simpler if there were more absolutes or certainties about the molds and marks used during her production. In fact, collectors have much good, solid information to help them identify authentic Bleuette dolls. But it remains important for collectors to continue to study and be aware that there are exceptions to many of the rules pertaining to Bleuette. After all, she was created as a mascot to increase sales of a magazine. She was not created with the concept that she would one day be collected and studied. She was the inspiration of businessmen who had a political agenda to espouse in their magazine for girls. The incredible appeal of Bleuette to several generations of French girls, as well as to collectors all over the world today, occurred after her production.

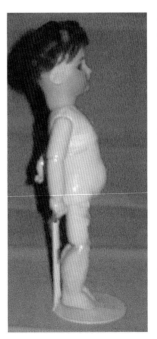

Far left: When shown side-by-side, these two Bleuettes from the 60 mold show distinct differences in their body construction and color. The SFBJ 60 8/0 on the left has a very typical body for a doll made in the "golden age" of Bleuette. Her companion on the right displays the very heavy calves found on some of the Bleuettes made before 1933.

Center: From the side, the 6/0 has an almost pregnant-looking, protruding stomach. The body is well balanced and assumes natural poses easily.

Left: Another 60 poses in a side view. Note the angle of the back of the knee to the calf. In spite of the very protruding stomach, the body is quite compact.

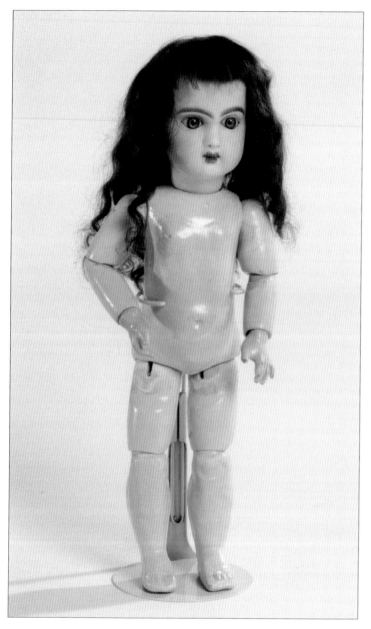

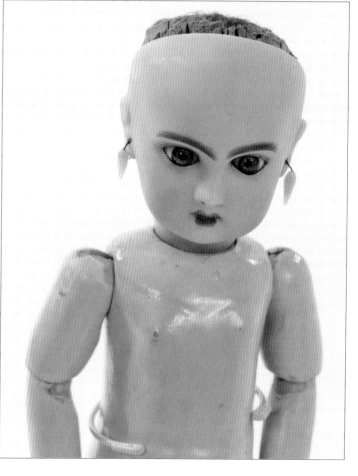

Above: The Première Bleuette has a sturdy, nicely proportioned body that suggests she can almost balance on her own. The composition and wood body of this Première is in remarkably good condition for a doll made in 1905.

Above right: you can just glimpse the pink drop earrings this lucky Première is wearing. Pierced ears are not routine with Bleuettes, but many do have them. The Première usually has very wide, strongly painted eyebrows and almost almond shaped eyes. The mouth is painted a true red with a coral undertone.

Right: When the wig is removed, you can observe the very steep forehead on this Première. Her pretty earrings show clearly in this photograph. The Première Bleuette should have a cork pate, if she is all original. Part of the unique beauty of each of these dolls is the specific way she is painted. The curve of the eyelashes, the width of the eyebrows, the focus of the eyes, the size and expression of the mouth—all these create the highly individualized look of each Bleuette.

CHAPTER

5

FAMILY MEMBERS AND FRIENDS

No book about Bleuette would be complete without discussion of the other members of her family, who were introduced over the years in the pages of the magazine. The additional family members invited girls to experience a variety of play options. Over a period of years, Bleuette was joined by a baby sister named Benjamine, a baby brother named Bambino and an older sister named Rosette.

BENJAMINE

Bleuette's first sibling, the darling Benjamine, was announced in *La Semaine de Suzette*, Issue 7, March 18, 1926. She was also shown in the Gautier-Languereau catalogs of that year. This sweet-faced baby has a porcelain head, mold SFBJ 251. She has sleep eyes and a bent-limbed composition body, which was described as being plump in the Spring 1926 catalog. The illustration for Benjamine in the catalog shows two infants sitting side by side. One is wearing a white pique dress; the other wears a romper crocheted by hand in rose or blue wool. Benjamine was also sold in a white crocheted costume, complete with a bonnet tied with silk ribbons. The bib Benjamine wore was also crocheted and edged with threaded silk ribbon "beading."

This precious little baby was expensive, compared to Bleuette. The initial offering of Benjamine in the mag-

This SFBJ 60 8/0 wears a vintage cotton print dress, which may have been homemade. She has a replaced mohair wig.

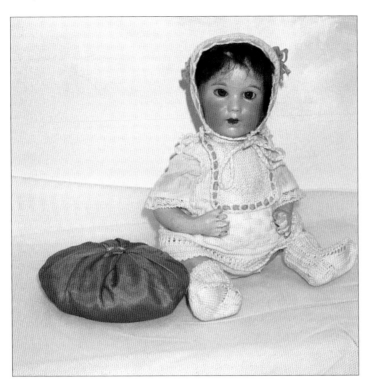

Bleuette's first sibling was Benjamine, a beguiling infant with an SFBJ 251 head, and a curved-limb infant's body. The doll was introduced in 1926, but never even came close to enjoying Bleuette's instant success. In the year of her introduction, another firm patented the names "Benjamin" and "Benjamine" for dolls, so Gautier-Languereau were forced to withdraw this darling baby from the market. Pictured is an all-original Benjamine. Her head is marked "SFBJ 251 2."

azine listed her price as 25 francs, compared to Bleuette's price of 14.50 to 17.50 francs at that time. Benjamine was produced for a very short time, and did not ever become really popular, possibly due to her high price. Another possible reason for her short production period is that she quickly ran into difficulty when another dollmaking firm accused Gautier-Languereau of stealing the name of their doll. George Lang had patented the name of Benjamin and Benjamine in 1929. The name Benjamine was dropped, and production of the doll ended. Whatever the true reason, because the doll was made for only a short time, she is rarely found today. (Amazingly, even after this problem with another dollmaker's copyright, Gautier and Languereau did not copyright the name "Bleuette" until October 2, 1935.)

At the Colonial Exposition of 1931, Gautier-Languereau introduced a little black friend for Bleuette The doll was named Bamboula. It has dark inset eyes, kinky painted hair, very dark skin, and wears only a simple ethnic skirt. This doll is not marked and measures 25 centimeters (9-7/8 inches) in height. It has a composition baby body and bent limbs.

BAMBINO

Bleuette's most popular sibling was her baby brother, Bambino, whose birth was announced in *La Semaine de Suzette* Issue 43, October 25, 1928. He was more successful than Benjamine, but never really approached the popularity of Bleuette. Introduced as a character baby, he was expensive, selling for about 55 francs. Although this was triple the cost of Bleuette, Bambino immediately found an eager audience. (It is worth noting that Bambino was offered at a time when character baby dolls from Germany were being eagerly sought in Europe and the United States.)

During the Colonial Exposition in 1931, Gautier-Languereau introduced a little black brother of Bambino, named Bamboula. He was produced only briefly and is very difficult to find today.

Left: A second, more successful baby sibling for Bleuette was introduced in 1928. His name was Bambino. Over the years, many patterns for a very complete wardrobe for Bambino were printed in La Semaine de Suzette. The catalogs also featured numerous layette items, so that Bambino could join Bleuette in all her adventures. This Première Bambino is shown in his presentation case, which includes a knitted layette. The interior of the case is lined with pale-blue, fine lawn edged with delicate lace and silk ribbons. Bambino always has painted hair. This example has a head of beautiful, oily bisque, and a composition body.

Above: It is rare indeed to find an all-original Bambino in his presentation case. This is the exterior of the case shown at the left. Note the sturdy construction and metal plate awaiting the engraver's touch to put the child's name on her luxurious gift.

When first issued, Bambino was 25 centimeters tall (9 1/4 inches), with bent limbs and a chubby baby body. He has almost no neck, just like a real baby. His body is the same as that used for Benjamine: a typical SFBJ baby body, with a straight back and rounded tummy. There is a hole in the base of his neck in front through which a string can be passed to limit the lead counter-weight of the sleep eyes. In addition, the body features a button-hip articulation. The thighs appear to have rolls of fat as part of the mold. His baby feet are nicely detailed with an up-turned big toe. When Bleuette increased to 29 centimeters, Bambino grew to 26 centimeters. Later still, in 1957, Bambino grew again to 27 centimeters.

Bambino is a bit of an enigma. Because the first Bambino was 25 centimeters, this suggests that the number 1 incised on the back of his head is meant to indicate his size, using the German numbering system. He is also clearly related to the German character babies with dome heads. The first Bambino looks very much like the mold 351 baby made by Armand Marseille. He has the domed head with softly "blushed," painted hair, an open mouth, two tiny teeth, and very small sleep eyes. Some researchers have suggested that A. Marseille may have manufactured this supposedly French baby brother for Bleuette. It is worth noting that the advertising for Bambino did not mention his country of

manufacture, unlike the advertising for Bleuette, who was always promoted as entirely French-made. Whatever his country of origin, Bambino captured the hearts of many little French girls, just as his sister Bleuette had done for many years.[34]

The first Bambino heads of very fine bisque are marked with a 1. This baby has an open mouth with tiny teeth. His hair is painted a soft reddish-brown and his eyebrows are delicately shaded lines. He has painted upper and lower eyelashes. His sleep eyes are cut very small.[35]

The second Bambino has a bisque head marked with a 3. He came with either a closed or open mouth; the open mouth has two teeth. He has sleep eyes, strongly painted triple-stroke eyebrows, and a very red mouth with a separate tongue.

Ultimately, there were five different models of Bambinos. All have molded hair, softly painted on the head, similar to the way blush is applied to doll cheeks. Beginning with the third version, the eyes were opened more and appeared more rounded in shape. The mouth continued to be painted a nearly garish red color. The final doll had a plastic or celluloid head, marked Jumeau-278/3. This doll some-

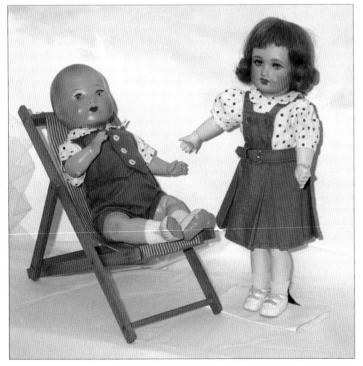

Top left: Another early bisque-headed Bambino reclines in his charming cradle. These cradles were used for both Bleuette and Bambino. They were made of study press-board and featured a slotted construction, allowing them to be flattened for storage. The designs painted on the sides and end of the cradle were created by artist Maggie Salcedo, who also illustrated some of the Gautier-Languereau catalogs.

Above left: A trio of Bambinos includes, from left: an all-celluloid late-production Bambino wearing a knitted yellow romper and cap featuring tiny "ears;" a bisque-headed Bambino, wearing a smocked dress and bonnet ensemble; a Bambino wearing a white knit outfit with booties. His head is porcelain; he is the earliest of these Bambinos.

Left: Frequently, matching outfits were sold for Bleuette and Bambino. Here, a 301 Bleuette and celluloid Bambino wear versions of "Don Desperado."

times has real eyelashes instead of the painted ones of the earlier models.

Bambino came fully dressed in a white hand-knitted ensemble. He was later sold undressed, too. Immediately, patterns for a very complete layette began appearing in *La Semaine de Suzette*. In all, seventy-five patterns were published for Bambino.[36]

The Gautier-Languereau catalog also featured numerous charming ensembles for all of his adventures. Many knitted ensembles were shown. Some were simple romper suits, while others had long leggings to keep the baby warm in winter. Bambino had patterns for bibs, a bath blanket and a set of combination underwear. He was well-equipped for sleeping, with various nightgowns and pajama sets. He had bonnets, caps and several two-piece bloomer-and-top outfits in various cotton fabrics. Rompers for Bambino were in the classic, puffed-sleeve, smocked-yoke and gathered-shorts style. Bambino also loved to swim, judging by the number of swimsuits that were offered.

Although Bambino was a little boy, he had numerous dresses and aprons. He also had several styles of sailor outfits, just like Bleuette. He was well prepared for winter with woolen coats and caps. Of course, he also had

Above: Bambino is ready for bed in "DoDo, l'enfant do." This pajama is made of shirting, decorated with blue-on-white woven ribbon and was shown in Gautier-Languereau catalogs from 1952-55.

Right: RoseAnn Wells made the cap and romper worn by this softly painted reproduction Bambino.

Left: This Bambino bears the marking "3," and wears a short creped cotton dress in a late 1950s style.

Above left: Another celluloid Bambino is shown with two classic costumes. He is wearing "Groeland," 1953-54 and 1954-55. The little sailor suit is called "Trésor," 1958-59.

Above: Bambino poses with his basinette and beautifully hand-smocked bonnet and dress. He is wearing a quilted Gautier-Languereau robe called "Mon Beau Bébé," 1935-36.

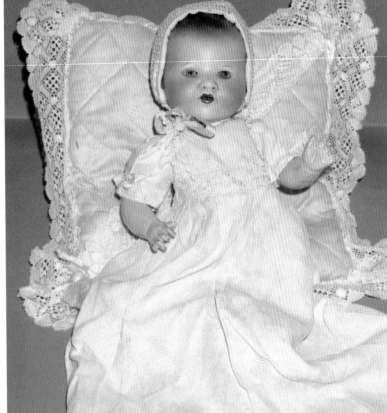

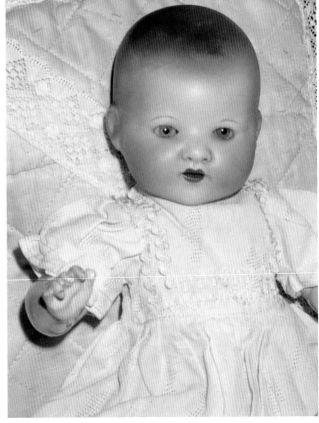

Above and right: Bambino had several different faces, just like his sister, Bleuette. This Bambino is marked "3" on the neck. He has rich, though delicate painting, on a bisque head. His sleep eyes are more rounded than almond in shape; he has no teeth in his open mouth. This Bambino is from the third edition. He wears a Baptismal gown and cap of mousseline, accented with ivory-colored silky rick-rack on the bonnet and bodice, from the Gautier-Languereau 1952 catalog.

Right: This interesting little summer frock is based on the costume called "Croquingnolette" from 1937-1939. Although the garment is clearly a dress, and Bambino was Bleuette's little brother, he had a number of short dresses for play and dressing up. The Gautier-Languereau costume is embellished with variegated, blue grosgrain ribbon rick-rack. The dress is made of a stretchy textured boucle-type fabric in off-white. This model is marked "3" on his neck.

Above: Bambino is ready for brisk weather in his knitted wool "Burnous," which was featured in the Gautier-Languereau catalogs from 1930 to 1936.

Right: Bambino is also available in reproduction form. These cute boys are all dressed and ready to play.

Some Bambinos seem to be almost garishly painted, by our modern standards. But for the girls who grew up with vividly colored Bambinos, the higher coloring is very desirable. This reproduction baby is wearing an old doll gown and hand-knit sweater. The reproduction Bambinos are 25 centimeters.

rain capes to keep him dry. This lucky little baby must have enjoyed skiing; he had several different ensembles for ski trips. One of the most enduring and popular of Bambino's costumes is his baptismal robe. This lovely long dress came in several versions, with a lace-edged and ruffled bonnet. The first gown in 1930 was covered with delicate embroidery and had a silk sash, but the dresses were soon made in a more tailored style with simpler lines.

Gautier-Languereau also offered furniture and a carry case for Bambino, as well as patterns in the magazine with instructions for making similar items. Examples of the furniture available included a green collapsible cradle, a hooded fabric-covered bassinet, sling chairs, and a playpen, complete with colorful wooden bead trim.

ROSETTE

Bleuette's older sister was not introduced until 1955. In the Spring-Summer catalog of that year, she was announced as a "great new thing"—a Bleuette that was 35 centimeters tall (13-7/8 inches). She was to arrive dressed only in her chemise, just like Bleuette. Her wig choices were rayon curls or natural hair braids. The wardrobe items available for her had the same names as similar dresses for Bleuette, and they looked very similar. She had a lovely bisque head, sleep eyes and an open mouth. She came on a fully jointed SFBJ body, and her

Opposite page: Rosette is ready to work in the garden. The aprons were made by Joyce Coughlin from patterns in La Semaine de Suzette. *From left: "Petite Tabliers pour notre jardinière" (little aprons for our gardener) # 22, 1929; "Tablier de maison," (house apron) # 33, 1912; "Tablier de jardinage," (gardening apron) #34, 1921. The appliqued design for this apron is shown in "Petite blouse fleurie," # 29, 1933.*

Far left: Rosette enjoyed all the same sports that Bleuette did. She is ready for a trip down the slopes in her "Slalom" costume from Winter 1949-50.

Left: Rosette, Bleuette's older sister, has a Unis France 301 head in either bisque or composition. This beautiful Rosette is wearing "Croisillons," from the Gautier-Languereau catalog, Winter 1957-58. She is marked Unis France 301, with a 3 on her neck indicating her larger size. She is 33 centimeters tall.

This charming Bécassine depicts our heroine when she is a young child; this is indicated by her red and white window-pane apron. All Bécassines are associated with their little bundles in red, or red and white, and with a red goose-head umbrella. Sadly, the umbrella is often the first item misplaced. All modern Bécassines are produced under license with Gautier-Languereau.

head was marked "Unis France."

When introduced, Rosette cost 1,875 francs for the model with a porcelain head and rayon hair, and 2,225 francs for a model with natural hair in braids. She was also available with a composition head for 1,800 francs with rayon hair, or 2,100 francs with natural hair. This doll was available for five years, although she never approached Bleuette's popularity. The name Rosette was not used until the Winter 1955-56 Gautier-Languereau catalog.

Patterns for Rosette were offered in *La Semaine de Suzette*, and she had her own page of fashions in the Gautier-Languereau catalogs. In Spring-Summer 1956, her trousseau items included: twenty-three dresses; a hat; a First Communion dress; and a long nightgown. A variety of shoes and stockings completed her toilette.

BÉCASSINE

In addition to the extended family of dolls surrounding Bleuette, Gautier also introduced a delightful comic character early in the publication of *La Semaine de Suzette*. Her name is Bécassine. Of all the dolls in the Bleuette circle, Bécassine probably enjoyed the most exposure because of the many stories written about her escapades. Chapters of her story were printed in comic strip form in *La Semaine de Suzette* throughout the years. She was also the heroine of a long series of children's books published by Gautier-Languereau, which are currently undergoing a renaissance. (The current books are published by Hachette Livre, today's owners of Gautier-Languereau.)

Bécassine was created almost by accident. Maurice Languereau invented Bécassine when a co-worker failed to produce a story for the back page of *La Semaine de Suzette*. The first story was quickly written by Jacqueline Riviere and illustrated by J.P. Pinchon.[37] Pinchon's huge contribution was to give the little heroine her distinctive shape and appearance. Later stories were written by Maurice Languereau, under the pen-name of "Caumery." The stories featuring Bécassine were written in comic-strip form for *La Semaine de Suzette*, usually filling the two center pages. The books published by Gautier-Languereau were large format, with the story told in the familiar comic-strip style. Over the long period of production, other

The heroine of so many stories and books associated with La Semaine de Suzette, *Bécassine* remains popular today. The tall doll in the rear is made of silk stockinette. Her features are painted. The cap is stitched to her head. The wool felt costume is edged with black velvet ribbon. Her "stockings" are strands of yarn wrapped around the legs to suggest stockings. The brown wool felt shoes are stitched in place. She carries a red-and-white checked gingham bundle, which matches her simple petticoat. Her costume is completed with lace-trimmed pantalons and a white work apron. She is 32 centimeters tall. This doll is the oldest in this group.

The small Bécassine with her hand in the bowl is made of a rubberoid plastic. She also wears wool felt clothing. Her stockings and shoes are painted. She has a loop in back so that she can be used as an ornament. She is 14 centimeters tall.

The seated Bécassine was made in 1955. She is dressed much the same as the tall Bécassine. The major difference is that her costume is made from soft wool challis instead of wool.

The porcelain bowl is in current production by Tropico Co. in Paris. Bécassine images decorate all manner of objects that are used in daily life.

An important aspect of Bleuette's popularity are the wonderfully entertaining, brightly colored books that have been published by Gautier-Languereau since the early 1900's. This display at the Exhibition in the Musée de la Poupée was held in February 2000.

writers were involved in creating the Bécassine stories. Additional artists were sought out, but their illustrations of Bécassine were not well accepted. J.P. Pinchon, who was the house artist for Gautier-Languereau, created an idealized version of Bécassine, with a completely round head, simple eyes and mouth, as well as a very tiny round little nose. His image of Bécassine was to endure throughout the years, even into the twenty-first century.

Bécassine is a young housemaid from Brittany. Her real name is Annaïck Labornez, but she is far better known by her nickname, Bécassine. A *bécassine* is actually a small, woodland bird found in France. The bird is supposedly rather stupid and clumsy. Sadly, the "heroine" of the Bécassine stories was very similar to her namesake!

In the background story, Bécassine leaves the village of Clochers les Bécasses to become a housemaid/nanny in the home of Madame de Grand Air. Bécassine's adventures are highly amusing, especially to children who often find themselves in similar predicaments. Always, Bécassine is portrayed as not-quite-bright, clumsy and accident-prone. An old wives' tale claims that one's intelligence is directly related to the size of one's nose—and Bécassine has a nose the

Below: This is just a small portion of the large Bécassine display at the Bécassine Luncheon given at UFDC in Chicago. Attendees quickly saw what a great variety of objects have been made to celebrate Bécassine. Guest speaker was Andrew Tabbat, who brought a large Raggedy Ann costumed as Bécassine, suggesting that these two beloved cloth dolls of childhood are truly "sisters" in the joy they have given.

Bécassine, costumed as an adult, is all set for a new adventure. She carries her bright red umbrella with the goose-head handle, and her perky checked bundle of goodies. The doll is made by Masport, in France, and is designed for safe play for very young children. The head is vinyl in this modern version. In past decades, her head was made of wood, composition, metal, cloth, or a rubber-like material.

A favorite of collectors is the little SFBJ 251 doll. There has been much discussion as to whether this doll was ever sold as a Bleuette. She is 27 centimeters tall and is frequently seen dressed in a Bécassine costume. Shown is a 251 doll with a composition head, dressed in her original Bécassine costume. She stands beside a catalog also featuring Bécassine.

From October 1999 through February 2000 the Musee de la Poupée in Paris held an exhibition called, "Bécassine, Bleuette et les poupées de La Semaine de Suzette." An entire room was filled with displays of Bécassine, including this enormous example, which is lawn bowling with a set of Bécassine "pins."

size of a pea! Bécassine always finds herself beset by difficulties, which she tries to solve using her own simple logic and genuine kindness. She travels widely in the stories, even making a memorable journey to the Wild West in the United States. Gautier-Languereau continues to issue reprints of twenty-seven of the early books. There are more than eighty newer books published in various formats—block and cloth books for the youngest children pop-up books; hard-bound and paper-bound editions; and books in the shape of Bécassine's famous Yellow Torpedo car. Her stories appeal to girls and boys alike. She has delighted successive generations of French children, much as Raggedy Ann does in this country.

Costumes for Bleuette to dress up as Bécassine helped increase the interest in the comic character when she was first created. Ready-made costumes were offered in every issue of the Gautier-Languereau catalogs. In addition, patterns for making a Bécassine costume were published in *La Semaine de Suzette* in 1908 and again in 1959. The later pattern included pattern pieces marked to make a Bécassine costume for either Bleuette or for her larger sister, Rosette.

Bécassine dolls were available through the catalogs, and continue to be produced today. They have been made from wood, porcelain, rubber, metal, cloth and vinyl. Her image has been used to decorate school bags; linens for teatime; games; dinnerware; silverware; picture frames; wagons; needlework of all sorts; and full-size clothing. Porcelain charms meant for baking into the traditional French Epiphany cakes were also made representing tiny, one-inch-high Bécassine figurines. Another set of charms has pictures of Bécassine on tiny porcelain squares. These Epiphany pieces continue to be produced today.

Bécassine's costume has remained much the same throughout her history. The dress is a style that was identified as Bretonne, of dark-green wool or heavy cotton. The bodice has a white plastron (a bib-like section of the bodice) with a black-ribbon-edged simulated apron bib of red. The long sleeves are green with a stripe of black ribbon. The skirt is also green, with a wide black ribbon at the hemline. A jaunty apron in stiff white fabric is tied at the waist, covering the front of the skirt. If the doll depicts Bécassine as a young girl, the apron is made of red-

and-white fabric in a windowpane design, rather than the plain white. She wears red-and-white knit stockings. Other accessories that are part of her costume include her red umbrella with a goose-head handle, and a small bundle wrapped in red-and-white checked fabric. The umbrella is featured first in *L'Enfance de Bécassine*, published in 1913. When she acquires the umbrella, she quickly wraps it in newspaper so it won't get wet![38] Bécassine's shoes are scuffs made of felt for indoors, and wooden clogs for trips outside. The distinctive headdress is made of starched heavy linen or cotton, with "wings" that stick out on either side.

This is Bécassine's traditional garb. However, she also has fancy lace-edged aprons and elaborately embroidered scuffs for serving at fancy parties. Although the forest-green was commonly used for the dress, occasionally a Bécassine is found with a dress of a different color. Sometimes the ensemble includes a red-and-white checked slip under the dress.

One of the interesting aspects of Bécassine's story is that she was at least partially involved with the introduction of babies into the Bleuette family. In 1921, Maurice Languereau and his wife became the parents of a baby girl named Claude. As a proud parent and the father of a little girl, Languereau soon introduced a young girl into the Bécassine story line. Madame de Grand Air adopted a small girl named Loulotte, and chose Bécassine to be her nanny. Shortly after Loulotte was introduced in *La Semaine de Suzette*, she appeared in the 1921-22 Winter catalog as a tiny baby in a baptismal gown. The next catalog also featured a baby. Then, in 1926, Benjamine was introduced as Bleuette's baby sister. By 1928, Bleuette's baby brother had been introduced. Although Bleuette does not actually appear in the Bécassine story, there are many connections between the two heroines and the magazine.

This large Bécassine, by Minerva, is taking care of a reproduction doll dressed in a beautiful Bécassine costume, designed and hand-knit by her owner, Beatrice Dockter. The costume is completed with an organdy cap and lace-edged apron in batiste. She wears sturdy wooden clogs. The doll was the souvenir at the first Bleuette Luncheon at the 1998 National Convention of the United Federation of Doll Clubs (UFDC).

PART II THE WARDROBE

The costumes shown on these pages are described on page 175.

6

PATTERNS IN *LA SEMAINE DE SUZETTE*

From the very beginning, the major focus of Bleuette was always her wardrobe. Not only is Bleuette's wardrobe one of the most extensive belonging to any doll ever produced, it is also acknowledged for the consistently high quality of the materials, accessory pieces and sewing skills employed in the creation of the garments. As we've discussed earlier, the purpose behind the girls' magazine, *La Semaine de Suzette*, was politically motivated and Bleuette was conceived as a premium to entice girls to desire and subscribe to the new magazine. The publishers realized, too, that to sustain continued interest in Bleuette and the magazine, the on-going publication of new patterns and the production of ready-to-wear clothing was needed.

Furthermore, in order to set Bleuette and her wardrobe apart from the standard dolls and clothing available at the time, Gautier-Languereau insisted that the clothes be made to real-people fashion standards. All trims, closures, etc. were to be in scale with the small doll. Materials were to be of the latest colors and finest fabrics. The styles, whether drawn as patterns in *La Semaine de Suzette*, or stitched by skilled seamstresses, were always in the very best taste and latest *haute-couture* styles. As a result, Bleuette became a source of continually renewed delight for several generations of French girls. Today, avid adult collectors all over the

One of the most enduring styles for Bleuette, as well as for real little girls, is the sailor dress called Marine in France. The colors and styling changed slightly over the years, as well as season to season. This version is made in soft navy-blue wool, and was featured in the Winter 1920-1921 catalog. The collar is white with navy embroidery, as is the plastron. The costume could be ordered in navy-blue wool serge or in dark-blue jersey. The pleated skirt was attached to a sleeveless linen bodice, which was covered by the jacket. The beret and collar were accented with navy-blue ribbon. The following year the Marine costume was offered with either pants or the pleated skirt. This 27-centimeter model is marked "SFBJ 301 PARIS 1." She also has the numerals "222" on her head, suggesting she was made in 1922.

*Marcene Oxford made this "*Tablier d' écolière*" (school apron) from a pattern in* La Semaine de Suzette, *# 45-46, 1906.*

world seek these exquisitely made small replicas of costumes that reflect the ultimate in good taste at various stages in French history.

In the world of dolls, French-made doll clothing has always been sought after as the finest available. This may be due in part to an unusual competition amongst seamstresses in Paris. By 1912, SFBJ was sending completed dolls to Paris to be dressed, where young girls stitched costumes reflecting the latest styles. Prizes were offered for improvement and new innovations. The high quality of doll clothes made in France was thus assured. The makers of Bleuette's wardrobe carried this level of excellence a step further, creating costumes that were at the absolute cutting edge of current fashion throughout the period of her production.

Bleuette grew to be viewed as a fashion leader in a nation noted for its fashion expertise, style and good taste. The collector who wishes to see the difference between doll clothing made in the United States and in France need only go to the library and consult issues of *Ladies Home Journal* or *The Delineator* published from 1905 to 1912 to see the difference firsthand. While the clothing is similar in some respects, the American-made

*Bleuette needed several costumes for school, so Marcene Oxford stitched another "*Tablier d'écolière*" from* La Semaine de Suzette, *# 8, 1911.*

*By 1916, many of Bleuette's dresses had a straighter line, with less ruffles and flounces. Marcene Oxford created this beautiful "*Robe de Maison*" (house dress) from* La Semaine de Suzette, *# 1, 1916.*

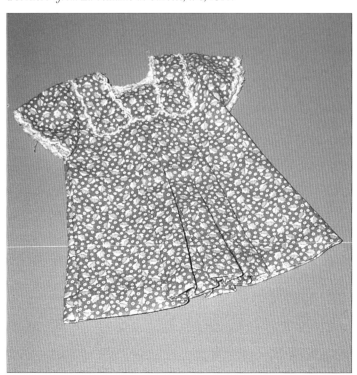

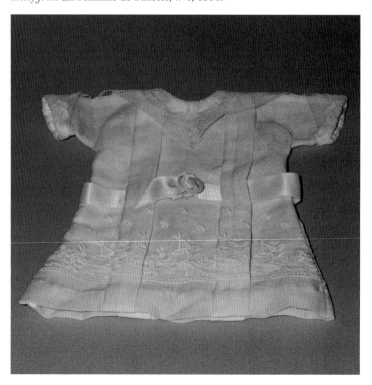

Right: Two versions of "Robe de Casino," demonstrate how effective small changes can be when using a basic pattern. The Première Bleuette on the right, wears the dress made from a pattern in issues #25-26, 1906, but without the bretelles and the flounce. The doll on the far right wears the "Tablier d'après-midi," 1905, over her Casino dress.

Right: The lovely "Robe de Casino," has been popular since it was first published. This vintage dress, with bretelles and flounce, is trimmed with antique silk ribbons.

Far right: Another version of the Casino dress, updated a bit, is worn by this relaxed 71 Unis France 149 301, 1-14. The dress is made from a deep blue-and-white waffle pique which gives the costume an over-all color of soft blue. Again, the bretelles and flounce have been eliminated.

garments are simplistic in line, and have a rather indefinite fit. The doll costumes appear to be simplified versions of the clothing made for real children.

The style sense of French women has been a much-admired trait for generations. Although they do not spend vast sums of money on their wardrobes, they manage to define understated elegance; each woman develops a style uniquely her own, achieved, in part, by building a wardrobe with a few basic pieces of excellent tailored clothing. To this foundation, they add the personal touches that imbue their wardrobe with high style: a colorful silk scarf; discreet but unusual jewelry; a well-fitted white shirt or silky blouse in a neutral color; a simple hair-do; make-up that emphasizes the lips and eyes. This unique appeal of understated elegance and classic style are very much a part of the success of Bleuette and *La Semaine de Suzette*. In this charming magazine, mothers found an ally to aid them in teaching their daughters the sense of style and high fashion so closely associated with French women.

Dressing Bleuette introduced girls to the wonders of each new sewing innovation as it was introduced. The primary closures on the Gautier-Languereau ready-made clothing were tiny hooks. These hooks were used from the mid-1840s to the present day, although the early ones were rather primitive and made of thin metal strands. Instead of a metal "eye," a simple loop made with hand-worked thread was often used. By 1892, a much-improved hook was available in various sizes. The ones used on Bleuette clothing were always in scale with the costume.

Elastic was available, but was not widely used until after elastic thread was invented. In the *Gazette de la*

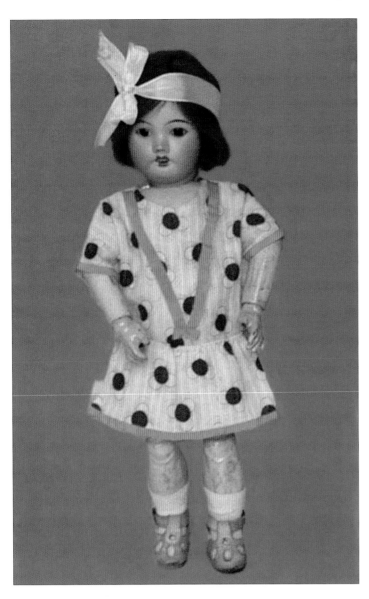

Another very popular pattern is "Robe Habillée" from issue #18, 1926. Bleuette 6/0 looks very stylish with the dramatic deep V design on the bodice and large polka dots. This is another dress that offers infinite variety, depending on fabrics used. Inside the dramatic V, a contrasting fabric can be used to create a very different look.

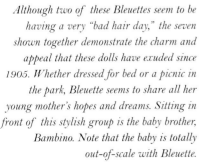

Although two of these Bleuettes seem to be having a very "bad hair day," the seven shown together demonstrate the charm and appeal that these dolls have exuded since 1905. Whether dressed for bed or a picnic in the park, Bleuette seems to share all her young mother's hopes and dreams. Sitting in front of this stylish group is the baby brother, Bambino. Note that the baby is totally out-of-scale with Bleuette.

Poupée, hat straps and insets on the sides of boots are mentioned as being used for dolls' clothing in 1867.[39]

For collectors trying to date a doll costume they find for sale, or trying to dress a beloved antique doll in a style and fabric appropriate to her own time, excellent sources of information are paper dolls, magazines and fashion books of the era. These sources often detail the fabrics being used, as well as the most popular textures, colors and print designs. Bleuette, however, is a true treasure of a source for dating costumes. *La Semaine de Suzette* not only offered patterns for an extensive wardrobe for Bleuette, but Gautier-Languereau Publishing also began printing catalogs of ready-made clothing available for Bleuette in 1916, and continued to do so until 1960. Let's first examine the patterns.

Beginning with the first issue of *La Semaine de Suzette*, a one-or-two-page feature appeared in every issue called *Nous Habillons Bleuette* (We Dress Bleuette). Since Bleuette arrived dressed only in an inexpensive cotton chemise, the new owner had to set about creating a wardrobe immediately. In fact, the publishers of the magazine suggested that little girls who were fortunate enough to receive a Bleuette needed to immediately fashion a pretty dress for her so that they could quickly introduce their beautiful new, properly attired doll to their friends.

The first pattern, published in 1905, was for a *Robe de Maison*, or house-dress. By today's sewing standards, this pattern and those that followed weekly, were rather complex for a novice young seamstress and the instructions, printed under the pen name *Tante Jacqueline* (Aunt Jacqueline), were often far from complete. (As men-

In the first years of publication, the patterns in La Semaine de Suzette *were the same or very similar to the ready-made costumes sold by the firm Gautier founded. The first pattern, published on February 2, 1905, has been charmingly stitched by Suzanne Gautrot of Paris. She used vintage eyelet and ribbon to create this simple dress for the Première Bleuette. If the collector desires authenticity, the Première doll should be appropriately dressed in costumes made from the very earliest patterns.*

Over the years, the classical nautical costume was a favorite for Bleuette. The dresses were white in the summer and dark navy or navy and red in winter. These five Bleuettes are set for a day at sea—they even have their fishnets ready. They were offered for sale at a Galeries de Chartres auction in France in May 2000.

This lovely doll is not a Bleuette, but she enjoys wearing Bleuette's costumes anyway! The doll, a French DEP, is wearing the classic Bleuette costume, "La Robe Écolière," from the Winter 1927-28 Gautier-Languereau catalog. Ruth Brown recreated the dress in new fabric which closely matched the original. To complete this costume, the doll should also wear a black tie at her neck.

tioned in Chapter 3, it is often assumed that many mothers, nannies, and household seamstresses were called into duty as the creators of Bleuette's first outfits.) Compounding the problem for a novice seamstress was the fact that many of the patterns were not sized to fit Bleuette! The early patterns, especially, tend to make up to be far wider than Bleuette's little body. Of course, more experienced seamstresses know to make a muslin, or even paper, sample before cutting fabric when sewing a costume.

The first five issues of the magazine contained patterns; but this pace of production of patterns was not sustained. In the first year, approximately forty patterns were published. In the decades that followed, the patterns were sporadically printed, but at least twenty-five were offered in any one year. The more complex patterns often took several consecutive issues to complete, sometimes as many as four.

The patterns were printed as graphics in the pages of *La Semaine de Suzette*. The patterns were accompanied by instructions for making the garment and offered suggestions for fabrics, trims and colors. Each pattern included the pattern pieces, graphics illustrating the embroidery and finishing techniques required, and a sketch of the completed ensemble, usually on a young girl or doll. Often, the little reader was encouraged to seek scraps in the sewing room, rather than beg her mother for costly materials. In this way, the child was meant to develop a sense that good fashion involved not only the cutting and stitching of a garment, but also the clever use of colors, trims and fabrics. The lessons of thrift and making-do were very much a part of the sewing lessons presented in the magazine.

Today these instructions continue to teach a new generation of doll collectors. One of the appealing aspects of sewing for Bleuette is that most of her costumes can be made from a "fat quarter" of fabric. (A fat quarter is a piece 18 inches deep and one-half the width of the fabric, selvage to selvage. This makes the quarter yard "fatter," or more square than a regular narrow strip, one-quarter yard of fabric.) Many of the costumes are trimmed with embroidery rather than expensive laces. When lace and beautiful ribbons are required, the small amount necessary to complete a garment is not too costly. Since the clothing for Bleuette is traditionally all hand-sewn, Bleuette owners can work on the garments

Demonstrating again how differently two costumes from the same pattern can look, Ruth Brown made this simple tailored outfit for her 301 using the same pattern from issue #31, 1913, that is worn by the doll at right.

This embroidered felt jacket was made by Ruth Brown for her 301 from a pattern in issue #31, 1913, "Jaquette Kimono." Ruth used an embroidery pattern from La Semaine de Suzette. The dress pattern is from 1926. Ruth also made the charming dogs.

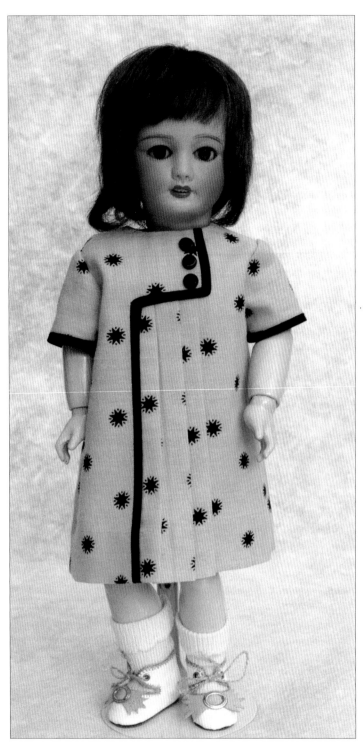

In 1926, "La Jolie Saison" was offered in the Spring-
Summer catalog. Ruth Brown has used vintage fabric
and trim to create her own version of this classic
dress. The Bleuette is a 71 Unis France 149, 301.

Bleuette, SFBJ Paris 60 8/0, is ready to play in her
romper of polished cotton. She has a mohair wig.

in almost any setting. Many find a great satisfaction in searching out vintage fabrics. Since only a small amount of fabric is necessary, even a torn or stained piece may offer enough unmarred fabric for a Bleuette costume. Women who enjoy hand-sewing often remark that the time and skill involved warrants working only with the very finest fabrics available. Bleuette's size permits this extravagance at a reasonable cost.

An examination of vintage home-made Bleuette garments reveals a great deal of imagination and innovation in the techniques used to create effects. For example, fabrics with a geometric print might be angled differently in separate areas of the costume, adding interest and texture to the final result. In the catalogs published by Gautier-Languereau, girls could see examples of the sorts of fabrics that could be used for the garments, and the manipulation of those fabrics in the many charming illustrations.

Opposite page, top: The gingham plaid silk in this dress has been sewn using some interesting, quick-sewing ideas that remain popular today. The hem-stitching is covered by contrasting silk ribbon, as is the edge of each puffed sleeve and the neck opening. The skirt is attached to the yoke in a clever way: First, the top edge of the skirt to be gathered is folded under. Then, when the skirt is placed next to the yoke for stitching, the skirt top, now gathered, actually covers the bottom edge of the yoke. With a double line of hand-stitching, the yoke and skirt are secured, adding a nice decorative note to the dress itself. The dress is closed with tiny white bead buttons, and thread loops. The center back seam is open to just past the waist, then finished in a French seam. The inside of this perky dress is as nicely finished as the outside!

Above: Bleuette was ready to help at a tea party wearing "Tablier pour Thé," (Tea Apron) which was stitched by Mathilde Hertier of Paris, from the pattern in issue # 16, 1925. Again, sharply contrasting color in the embroidered edging and binding are effectively used. Mathilde has stitched the costume to a presentation card, complete with a sketch from La Semaine de Suzette.

Right: "Graziella" was offered in blue or rose in the Winter 1933-34 catalog. The lovely model is an SFBJ 251.

Any study of Bleuette and her times must include a close study of the patterns offered in *La Semaine de Suzette*. The garments outfitted this little doll—and fired the imagination of her child "mama"—to undertake many adventures. In spite of the magazine's stated purpose to mold little girls to be the future mothers of France, it also had to appeal to thoroughly forward-looking young girls. As a result, as girls broke out of their formerly cloistered existence, Bleuette and her handmade wardrobe accompanied them each eventful step of the way into the future.

THE EARLY PATTERNS

The pattern pieces for the dress in the first *Nous Habillons Bleuette* feature were drawn in the most economical manner, with just a few lines and circles to indi

Using a pattern in La Semaine de Suzette, *issue #30, 1939, Ruth Brown has created this lovely formal gown for her Unis France 301, using vintage silk taffeta.*

One of the fascinating aspects of sewing for Bleuette is discovering how different the same pattern can look when stitched with different trims and fabrics. An example is the "Robe d'Été" (summer dress), pattern number 4, 1905, created by Louise Hedrick in vintage silk taffeta for the Première Bleuette. When the dress is made in white taffeta with a bright blue ruffled trim down the front, the look is quite different.

cate how to cut and stitch the dress. This first pattern for Bleuette featured simple cap sleeves, a dropped waist and a large bow both at the left shoulder and on the ribbon at the doll's hips. The skirt had a charming ruffle of fabric. The neckline was bound with bias made from the dress fabric. Pattern pieces were given for the bodice and sleeve, while only measurements were given for the skirt and its ruffle. There were simple patterns for Bleuette's *pantalons* (panties), embroidered stockings and laced shoes. These patterns, basic and typical of daily wardrobe needs for a young girl, set a model that *La Semaine de Suzette* would follow for the next fifty-five years.

The pattern pieces for some of the first costumes for Bleuette had such complexity of construction that several editions of *La Semaine de Suzette* were necessary to complete the outfit. The pattern for *Robe en Linon Fleuri*

Another Bleuette 6/0 wears "Robe Empire," from La Semaine de Suzette, *issue #17, 1908. She carries a purse in embroidered silver linen made by Mathilde Hertier of Paris, from* La Semaine de Suzette, *#12, 1911, and wears replaced shoes and socks.*

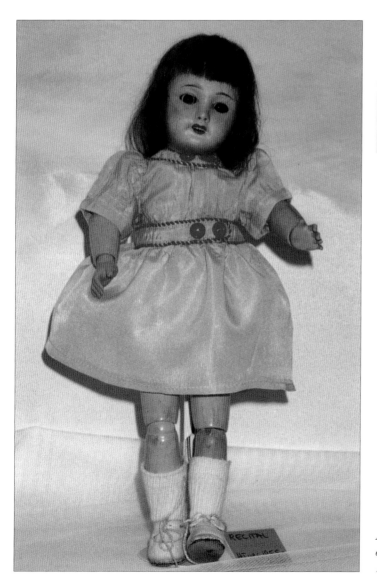

A pretty Unis France 301 Bleuette is ready to step out in her silk taffeta dress, "Recital," from Winter 1955-56 catalog.

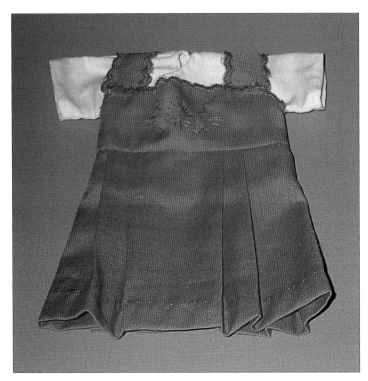

Note the careful same-color embroidery on this charming apron, made by Marcene Oxford from issue #25, 1918. Eyelet was created by hand in the early twentieth century. Judging by Bleuette's wardrobe, hand-embroidered eyelet (brodérie anglaise) was also very popular!

Since girls were to hone their sewing skills while making Bleuette's wardrobe, various embroidery techniques were taught in making many of the patterns. The girls also learned early that embroidery is an inexpensive way to achieve a beautiful decoration. Marcene Oxford stitched this "Robe de demi-saison," (light-weight dress), from issue #32, 1918.

Rose (dress in flowered rose linen), published in two consecutive issues, is a case in point. The softly gathered bodice and flared skirt with a deep flounce, gathered in tiny pleats every few inches at the hemline, would surely have challenged most beginning seamstresses! As was customary in the time of Edwardian fashion, the hemlines reached nearly to the ankle. The bodice and sleeves featured open, relaxed pleats that enhanced the softly feminine look of the costume. The neckline of the Rose Linen dress was completed with a large bow under Bleuette's chin. In 1907, the skirts on Bleuette's garments began to creep up to the level of her knee.

The costumes featured various types of embroidery techniques: *broderie anglaise* (hand-embroidered eyelet); scallops; braid-stitching with colorful patterns of fruit or flowers sewn to the dress; satin-stitching; application of soutache braid to lapels, sleeves and skirts; chain-stitching; stem-stitching; feather-stitching; French knots; blanket-knitting; and the making of fringe to edge a vest-top. Diagrams were carefully drawn to demonstrate how to form each embroidery stitch. Other techniques used included connecting ribbon with fagoting stitches to create an entirely new "fabric" for a dress. (Fagoting is a method of connecting the edges of two different pieces of fabric by criss-crossing thread over an open seam, or by pulling out horizontal threads and tying the remaining vertical threads into hour-glass-shaped bunches.) Ribbon rosettes and ruching were often used as decorative accents, as well. Beading was used to enhance the embroidery on the bodice and waistline of garments. Applique and lace insertion or edging were also taught in *La Semaine de Suzette*. Cross-stitching was used, as well as old-fashioned feather-stitching, to achieve unique decorative effects.

Always, Bleuette's patterns were for garments that real girls needed or wanted. There was a definite sense of practicality in the patterns, but also a sense of adventure. Some of the patterns were for clothing that only very well-to-do little girls might have needed. Additional early patterns were included for a chemise; a *capulet* or cloak; an extravagant hat in carefully stitched and edged straw; and many dresses. The mysteries of setting a round yoke onto a dress were unraveled. As early as the twenty-fifth issue of 1905, Bleuette was encouraged to be athletically active with her first swimsuit. Accessories were also introduced in the first year.

These included embroidered collars; a hatbox; a bib; a crocheted purse and scarf; a knitted skirt of wool; an open workbasket for sewing; and a pattern for "American" stockings, which appear to be simply stockings made of a fine cotton knit material.

THE LAYETTE

Although Bleuette was definitely a little girl, not an infant, a set of patterns was offered in the early 1900s for a wonderful baby's layette. Perhaps the editors realized that some little girls would want to have Bleuette be a little baby, at least some of the time. These layette patterns were intended for Bleuette. Later, a number of patterns would be offered for Bleuette's baby brother, Bambino, but these later patterns are quite separate from Bleuette's layette designs.

Among the layette patterns offered were numerous embroidered and lace-edged bibs; a long under slip called a "layette Jackson;" a diaper cover; a belly band; a dress featuring *brodérie anglaise*; a long-sleeved short shirt called a *brassiere*; and a particularly beautiful Baptismal dress, coat with attached capelet, and a lovely bonnet. A pattern for dainty embroidered booties was also included. All of these patterns were published between 1905 and 1908!

In following years, more patterns were offered: a long day gown; additional chemises and corsets; more *brassieres* and a traditional *sacque*—a little short jacket worn over an infant's undershirt. Patterns were also given in *La Semaine de Suzette* for Baptismal gowns, more booties and, of course, more diaper covers. Patterns for costumes for Bleuette as a baby are listed as "Layette" patterns, followed by the name of the garment. The layette patterns were published as part of *Nous Habillons Bleuette*.

SPORTS COSTUMES

One of the earliest costumes for Bleuette that suggested her enthusiasm for an active, athletic life was the bathing suit pattern published in 1905, issue number 25. In 1906, a more elaborate swimming suit was offered. The latter complete ensemble included a blouse that fell just below the hipline. It had a patriotic collar embellished with embroidered stars. The costume was completed with bloomers, a bonnet and bathing shoes.

The magazine provided patterns that allowed Bleuette to accompany her "mama" as they participated in various athletic activities. The most prevalent sporting costume

Marcene Oxford used soft vintage fabrics to create "Costume de Jeux," from issue #19, 1917.

Bleuette is all set for a day of fun at the ocean with two swimming suits (1915), two deck chairs, a changing cabana, and a "boater" straw hat, barely visible on the right, all made by Joyce Coughlin. Swimming suits (Costumes de bain) were included in various designs throughout Bleuette's production.

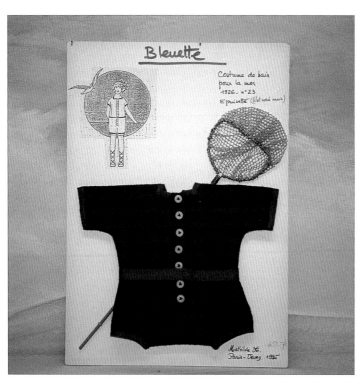

*A costume from issue #23, 1926, includes a fishing
net as well as* "Costume de bain pour la mer"
*(swimsuit for the sea). Mathilde Hertier of Paris
created this costume.*

was the swimming suit. Patterns in *La Semaine de
Suzette,* as well as regular offerings in the Gautier-
Languereau catalogs, suggest that Bleuette spent a lot of
time at the seashore. Since the first pattern for a *Costume
de Bain* in 1905, a complete history of girls' swimming
costumes in the first half of the twentieth century can
be found in the pages of *La Semaine de Suzette.*

The bathing costumes range from multi-layered,
elaborately made dresses with bloomers, to the sleek
look of the *maillot* style still popular today. The fabrics
recommended were fine woolens, heavy cottons and jersey, as well as various knits.

In 1915, Bleuette's swim outfit included patterns for a
belt, bathing shoes and a fishnet on a long pole. In 1919,
her swimsuit looked very modern, with tailored boy-leg
shorts and a sleeveless top. By 1921, the bathing costume had become a one-piece short-all with a v-neckline
and a gauze fabric cape, which was used as a cover-up.

Patterns for hooded capes and cover-ups were given.
In addition, there were patterns for *espadrilles*, meant
for walking on the beach. There was also a pattern for
sandals meant for playing in the sand. The variety of
patterns within a particular category, like swimwear,
gives us an excellent insight into the kind of lifestyle
Bleuette's owners enjoyed.

Bleuette participated in a wide range of sports. In
1907, a series of patterns offered a complete costume
for Bleuette's hunting trip. The jacket and pleated skirt
were tailored, with button-and-belt trim. A jaunty hat
with a feather was made from a deceptively simple-
looking circle of felt or heavy fabric. Her gaiters,
designed to protect her lower legs, laced up the sides
through holes sewn with buttonhole stitching. The gun
case for Bleuette's rifle was to be made from thin
leather. The ensemble was completed by a large bag for
carrying the game from the hunt. It featured a loose-
woven outer pouch, as well as the enclosed leather bag.
A second hunting costume has an interesting hat that

*This perky SFBJ 60 8/0 is ready for a day at the
seashore. She wears a* "Costume de bain" *called*
"Crevette" *(crab). The swimsuit was pictured in the
Gautier-Languereau Spring-Summer 1927 catalog,
and was also offered as a pattern in 1923. Over her
bathing costume, Bleuette wears* "Peignoir éponge"
(a swimsuit cover made of a gauze-like fabric).

resembles the early American patriots' hats.

In 1913, Bleuette was ready to go fishing in a navy costume with a floppy stocking cap, traditional wear for fishermen and women in France. The skirt and over-blouse had a nautical look, and jersey was the recommended fabric. The blouse was worn long, down to the hips. Long stockings completed this ensemble.

In 1928, Bleuette took up tennis in a pleated-skirt ensemble. Her costume was a neatly tailored, sleeveless dress with a pleated skirt, worn with a loose-fitting box jacket over it. White wool flannel was recommended for this pattern, which has seven parts. The lining for the jacket and sleeves was to be made of fine blue or red fabric. Bleuette's second tennis costume featured a pleated skirt and sleeveless top, plus a delightful cap with a fetching lattice-work design and a stiff bill.

In 1922, a knitted costume called simply *"Costume de Sport"* was offered. It was suitable for a lively game of croquet or other lawn sports. A charming pattern for long stockings with a decorative cuff at the knee was offered soon after.

The costumes for playtime were not the casual jeans and tee-shirts of today. Bleuette wore a blouse with dainty embroidery at the neck and on the cuffs of the sleeves. Over this, a loosely fitted romper gave her freedom of movement for play. The costume was secured by a belt that buttoned in front at the waist.

In the winter, Bleuette loved to skate. Over the years, patterns for several skating outfits were published. One of the first showed a full skirt to the knees, with a fur-trimmed long jacket and a warm fur mitt. Her toque hat was also fur-trimmed. When she tired of skating, Bleuette could take to the slopes in her warm ski ensemble, which included a pleated skirt and jacket embroidered with a floral motif.

In 1930 Bleuette took up fencing. This costume was cleverly designed, complete with a protective vest, and is rather challenging to complete. It includes the spe-

Since young girls love to pretend they are fine ladies, a beautiful gown was offered in La Semaine de Suzette. *"Robe de Soirèe" was presented in issues # 52-53, 1912. This elegant version was stitched completely by hand by Mathilde Hertier.*

A clever use of woven braid makes this apron particularly appealing. "Tablier d'Apès-midi," is from a pattern in La Semaine de Suzette, #40, 1912.

Ruth Brown has sewn this small piece of vintage fabric into a stylish dress for Bleuette. Creative use of contrasting trim continued to be an important design element. It also helped young seamstresses learn to "make do" with very small pieces of fabric. The model is a 71 Unis France 149, 301.

Vintage cotton makes even the newest dresses look appropriate for Bleuette. Ruth Brown made this colorful version of a pattern from the magazine in 1933.

cialized vest, with a red heart appliqued on the left chest, and buttons from the neck down the shoulder, around the armhole, and down the side of the vest to the left side of the waist. The skirt was to be made of finely pleated linen or wool and the vest of canvas. The entire costume was meant to be white.

For sailing, Bleuette could put on her two-piece shorts outfit with a lovely embroidered "B" on the bodice. For active play in the garden, she could wear a loose-fitting romper with a deep pocket at the waistline. The costume for paddling a canoe was similar to the sailing outfit, but included a billed cap and a fringed stole. For cycling, Bleuette's costume had a pleated skirt, short-sleeved blouse and ribbon tie at the neck and on the pocket. Costumes for golfing often included knitted sweaters over pleated or gored skirts. Obviously, all these activities required new strength, so a pattern was provided for Bleuette's weight-training and gymnastics. The costume for this sport was a loose-fitting sleeveless tunic over full gathered bloomers. In 1931, Bleuette could also go horseback riding in her tailored vest, jodhpurs and billed cap.

One of Bleuette's most adventurous costumes was published in November 1927. Bleuette proved she was a thoroughly modern and adventuresome girl with the publication of the *Bleuette Aviatrice* pattern: a flight suit with buttoned cuffs at the wrists and ankles. But the most exciting piece of this costume may have been the soft leather flight helmet, which included perforated rondels at the ears so Bleuette could "hear" what was happening. The pattern explained that these round pieces were made of metal in a real pilot's helmet, but for Bleuette, the ear pieces were to be made of several layers of fabric, stitched together with cotton perle thread. The holes were simulated by French knots. Suggested fabrics for the aviator's uniform were heavy-weight khaki cotton or very thin leather, such as kid skin.

LINGERIE

The patterns in *La Semaine de Suzette* for Bleuette's lingerie offer another glimpse of how the lives of girls were changing during the production of Bleuette. In the early years of the twentieth century, there were patterns for corsets made with stiffened and reinforced fabrics; chemises; combination underwear; pantaloons (long-legged panties), slips; and nightgowns. Sometimes, the early corsets were called "stays," if they were meant for a young child. There were also aprons or *tabliers*, for every sort of activity: helping in the kitchen; eating a meal; doing school work; and gardening. Very elaborate ones were meant for party occasions. A variety of bibs (*serviettes de table*) were also offered so that Bleuette would not soil her pretty dresses.

Among the many patterns for nightgowns (*chemises de nuit*) were elaborate confections of lace-trimmed gowns, simple night dresses, pajamas and traditional embroidered gowns. Dainty handkerchiefs were part of any girl's proper *toilette*. These small pieces of fine lawn or batiste offered opportunities for young girls to practice embroidery, *entredeux* lace, faggoting, and the application of delicate lace edgings.

In addition, Bleuette was encouraged to keep order among her belongings with the many cases, boxes, trunks and bags for which patterns appeared in *La Semaine de Suzette*. The bags meant for holding lingerie were delicately embroidered and edged with lace.

Another essential of a lingerie wardrobe are the robes, or *peignoirs*. These were usually made of lighter-weight fabrics trimmed with appliques or embroidery. *Peignoirs de bain* were similar to modern beach cover-ups. The first pajamas for Bleuette appeared in the catalogs of 1924, but were not introduced in pattern form in the magazine until 1933, in issue 11. Once introduced, patterns for pajamas were seen frequently in *La Semaine*

In addition to a concern that each costume be appropriate for the period when the doll was manufactured, Bleuette collectors also try to re-create the wide assortment of underwear that was presented in La Semaine de Suzette *and the Gautier-Languereau catalogs. This Bleuette 6/0 wears a slip made from a pattern in* La Semaine de Suzette, #38, 1916.

Bleuette had many wonderful pieces of lingerie, from the Gautier-Languereau catalogs as well as from La Semaine de Suzette. *Marvyle Walker's SFBJ Paris 301 models a charming nightgown embroidered with floral motifs drawn in the pattern in issue #9, 1933.*

A complete First Communion ensemble would normally include a small cross worn as a necklace and a small alms purse tied at the waist. This Unis France 301, with composition head, wears "Un Beau Jour" from Spring-Summer 1952.

de Suzette. This casually elegant nightwear looks particularly fetching on little girls, or on Bleuette dolls!

The combination underwear was presented in several forms. Some were essentially a chemise with a closure in the crotch that formed to create leg holes. Other examples had a simple gored skirt. A few had much more elaborate, tiered ruffles. Combinations were also made with short, boy-style legs or longer legs that almost covered Bleuette's thighs.

First Holy Communion

Since religion, specifically the Roman Catholic faith, was an essential part of the rationale for publishing *La Semaine de Suzette,* various costumes and accessories for significant holy days in a young girl's life were featured over the years. Baptismal gowns and long coats with capelets and fancy bonnets or caps were featured from the beginning. An important religious event in a girl's life that she was encouraged to act out with her Bleuette was *"Le Beau Jour"* (First Holy Communion).

Of great and continued importance in Bleuette's wardrobe was her gown for her First Communion. These dresses, always white, included a hat or lacey cap and a fingertip veil. At her waist, Bleuette carried her delicately made alms purse, called an *aumônière.* Costumes for this important day in a young girl's life were available in pattern form and in many issues of

Joyce Coughlin set up a beautiful little altar scene at her home in Bellevue, Washington. The Bleuette 60, 8/0 on the left and the Bleuette 6/0 on the right are both costumed in gowns and veils made by Joyce. She used delicate fabrics, and small-scaled laces to achieve the beautiful look of children at their First Communion. The "priest" is an unmarked German bisque doll, costumed by Joyce. She has collected all the miniature items on the altar over a period of years. Each item is authentic and in-scale.

*Even a brief study of documents pertaining to Bleuette offers
the insight that the Roman Catholic faith and its rituals were very
important in the lives of young girls. Bleuette celebrated her
First Communion (Le Beau Jour) in lovely gowns throughout her long
production. Patterns were offered in* La Semaine de
Suzette *for her gown, veil, alms purse, Missal cover, altar linens, and
various hats or elegant little capelets. The catalogs also included
beautiful selections for this very special day in a girl's life. This
lovely Unis France 301 is wearing a gown made of vintage organdy,
stitched by Louise Hedrick. She has a delicate veil with beautiful
edge-stitching. She carries a treasured antique miniature rosary.*

the Gautier-Languereau catalogs. The dresses were to be made of fine fabrics, such as organdy, and included a hat, a veil and the long gown. Decoration was usually limited to vertical pleats on the bodice and multiple rows of horizontal tucks on the lower skirt. The veil might be edged with delicate lace or a tiny ruffle. The alms purse was frequently embroidered with the young Communicant's initials.

In addition to the dress for this special day, patterns were included in the magazine for various accessory pieces: dainty hankies; a prayer book or Bible cover; a runner for the table to be used at the reception following the First Communion; and a number of different hats and veils. The young girl preparing for her First Communion might embroider the date on a handkerchief, along with suitable symbols of the day, such as a cross, an anchor, and a heart. Embroidered silk stockings and dainty slipper shoes completed the costume.

OUTERWEAR

Beginning in 1905, Bleuette's owner was urged to make plenty of warm stylish coats and jackets for her favorite doll. The first jacket presented was to be

Above left: The main decorative design for this lovely SFBJ Paris 301's Communion dress is tiny tucks taken in the bodice, and deeper tucks around the skirt. The gown is made out of crisp white organdy, as is the veil. A bonnet, securing the veil and tying under the chin, completes the ensemble. The dress is from Gautier-Languereau, 1952.

Far left: Bleuette is ready for spring showers in her pretty blue raincoat, called "Averse," from Winter 1939-40. She is carrying a "Sac d'école," which was given in a pattern in issue #45, 1910.

Left: This SFBJ 251 with composition head is wearing the popular "La Rafale" coat from the Spring 1928 catalog.

This costume was shown at a special exhibition honoring Bleuette and Bécassine at the Musée de la Poupée, Paris, 2000. The ensemble is "Robe brodée en laine" stitched by Suzanne Gautrot, from issue #51, 1918, and issue # 2, 1919.

This sweet-faced 71 Unis France 149, 251, 2, is wearing a cape called "Vêtement de demi-saison," (light-weight cape) from La Semaine de Suzette, *issue #16, 1924. The doll is 29 centimeters tall and has a "2" on her back and a "1" on the sole of each foot.*

made from a light woolen fabric, in beige, grey, olive-green, red or French blue—the fashionable colors in 1905. The red color was recommended as being the favorite of children. The second pattern for a coat was more complex, and featured five pattern pieces, which created a coat with a two-piece front, wide yoke, narrow band and gathered back-piece for a very stylish look.

Many patterns were offered for raincoats over the years. Girls were encouraged to use sturdy, water-repellent fabrics for these essential wardrobe items. Bleuette also enjoyed outerwear made in styles that celebrated other cultures. In 1907, she wore a coat and toque-style hat in the Japanese mode. In 1919, a pattern was offered for an American-style coat. In case old fur was available, patterns for fur coats, muffs, collars and trims for sleeves and coat fronts were offered.

In addition to long coats, patterns for short, tailored jackets were also given. Patterns for many different capes with hoods or coats with capelets built into the garment were published. Some of the capes were clearly meant to be worn at the beach over bathing suits. Other capes were made with a fringe or other embellishments that offered girls a chance to learn new embroidery techniques. An example is the dainty, ruffled cape that is simply called the flounced coat, published in 1923.

Of course, there were numerous coats and jackets to be worn on trips or the walk to school. Bleuette also wore many decorative vests. Some of the vest patterns were included as part of a dress pattern. Others were presented as a simple way to expand Bleuette's wardrobe. The vests could be made of any fabric. Some were lined. But several were cut from simple felt, edged with a blanket-stitch and trimmed fabric rondels matching the print of the dress.

Additional outerwear patterns were offered for gloves; mittens; boots; gaiters; and heavy stockings. There were also many patterns for knitting and crocheting hats, scarves and sweaters to keep Bleuette warm.

CROCHET AND KNITTING

Throughout the years of publication, *La Semaine de Suzette* included patterns for knitting and crocheting costumes for Bambino and Bleuette, as well as for various accessory pieces, such as hats, scarves, blankets, swimsuits, etc. There were probably more patterns for Bambino simply because he was a baby and traditional

The patterns in La Semaine de Suzette *regularly offered instructions for knitting and crochet work. The catalogs also offered completed knit costumes. This reproduction SFBJ #60 8/0 is wearing a bright blue-and-white knitted ensemble made in France in 2001, based on the costume "Golf," in the Winter 1920–1921 catalog. She holds her teddy bear and Dolly Dingle paper dolls.*

The early patterns for Bleuette were quite wonderfully feminine and dainty. A beautiful case-in-point is the "Chapeau de demi-saison," issue #9, 1906. Louise Hedrick used delicate silk chiffon to fashion this bonnet, with two lovely ribbon rosettes on either side of the tucked brim. The body of the bonnet features softly pleated tucks.

clothing for infants during the reign of Bleuette was frequently knitted. The crochet patterns were offered for blankets, Bambino clothing and purses or bags. Several hat patterns involving crochet work or knitting were also published.

HATS

Bleuette's hats are the subject of an entire book (Albert Bazin, *Les Chapeaux de Bleuette*, 2000). More than three hundred hats for Bleuette are offered in pattern form in *La Semaine de Suzette*, and in the catalogs published by Gautier-Languereau. Obviously, a well-dressed young lady needed to complete her toilette with the appropriate hat! In addition to hats that complemented costumes, there were hats that served special purposes—ranging from the leather helmet for the *aviatrice* (pilot) to sunbonnets for working in the garden. One of the earliest patterns, in 1906, included a special hat to be worn for traveling by automobile. Turned one way, the hat was a normal head covering. Turned 180 degrees, the brim of the hat could be lowered and there were holes through which the doll could "see" the road!

Definitely one of the most intriguing hat patterns in the magazine was for a hat to be worn while riding in an automobile. When not on the road, Bleuette could wear the jaunty hat high on her head. But when the automobile got under way, she could turn the hat around, pull the "bill" down, and watch the road through the gromet protected holes! The model is the Première Bleuette. The entire costume was stitched by Louise Hedrick in vintage fine wool, using patterns in issue #29-30, 1906.

Bleuette's hats ranged from jaunty berets to elaborate straw, silk and lace creations. Many costumes included a hat or the pattern for a hat. Then, there were more than 300 additional hats produced for this little fashion-conscious doll. One of the earliest is the stunning straw and silk creation named simply "Chapeau." The hat is in issue #11, 1905. This version was created by Louise Hedrick from vintage materials. Louise also created the matching dress in vintage silk and soutache from issue # 20-21, 1907. The beautiful model is a Première Bleuette.

Bleuette also had costumes for various occupations. One of these is the Costume of the Tramway Conductor. The pattern was offered in the magazine, #10-11, 1919; this rendition was made by Mathilde Hertier of Paris.

The "Costume d'Espagnole" is from issue #4, 1931. This example was also made by Mathilde Hertier of Paris.

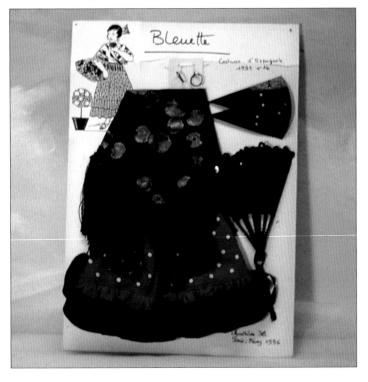

Each year multiple hat patterns were published for Bleuette. Some were clearly part of an entire ensemble. But there are also numerous patterns that could be worn with assorted costumes. Little girls were able to explore customs of other cultures by making the numerous headdresses that accompanied ethnic patterns from all over the world. The hat patterns used techniques ranging from embroidery and layered stitching, such as in straw hats, to knitting and crochet work in wool, to crocheting with paper twisted to form a sort of "yarn." Some of the hats were frankly military in origin of their design. Others were appropriate to certain professions, such as nursing, or being a nanny. Each sporting costume had its own appropriate hat. Some hats were suggested by the costume they were designed to enhance: *i.e.* Harlequine; Cendrillon—(Cinderella—a scarf tied under the chin); Pierrette and Pierrot; *Costume de Bain* (swimming cap); and Bécassine. Just as Bleuette's outfits had romantic names, so, too, did her hats. No matter what the inspirational source, however, Bleuette's hats offered ample opportunities for girls to learn additional sewing techniques.

ACCESSORIES

In addition to clothing for Bleuette's trousseau, the patterns in *La Semaine de Suzette* covered a wide range of items a young girl might find necessary to have for her doll. There were instructions for making furniture for Bleuette; bed linens; party decorations and favors; games; puzzles; purses; bookbags; small valises; stockings; shoes for all occasions; slippers; boots; and even a small rug to be made with a knitting spool. There were patterns for fans; umbrellas; dainty parasols; leather gloves; and lace mittens. Patterns for belts offered an opportunity for girls to practice various embellishment techniques with embroidery and soutache. Among the craft projects were a dainty woven basket and various styles of beaded bracelets, necklaces and earrings. Of course, all this jewelry meant there had to be a pattern for a jewelry box for Bleuette!

Bleuette could make all the hatboxes she needed for her huge wardrobe of hats, using a basic pattern from *La Semaine de Suzette*. She was also urged to create a workbasket of pretty fabric-covered cardboard, with special cushions and pockets stitched into the interior to accommodate pins, needles, thread and scissors. One

pattern from 1917 even shows how to make a little lamp so that Bleuette can read and sew in the evenings!

COSTUMES OR DÉGUISEMENTS

During the course of Bleuette's long production, many delightful costumes, or *déguisements*, were created for her. These were costumes to be worn to a party at which everyone was dressed in a make-believe manner. Bleuette was always a little girl, even though some of the costumes were obviously suitable for a more mature young lady. For example, during four different decades, lovely bridal gowns with headdresses and veils were published as patterns in *La Semaine de Suzette*. It is important to remember that these costumes were never intended to be for a child bride; rather, they were designed for some make-believe, dress-up fun.

Dress-up parties involving elaborate costumes and settings have a long tradition in France. Marie Antoinette even had an entire miniature village built so that she could dress as a country maiden and milk her immaculate cows! The tradition probably dates much further back than that. Since Lent, preceding Easter in the church calendar year, is a time for solemn intro-spection, gala parties and parades often preceded the season of Lent, or took place at a time of celebration in mid-Lent. (In the United States, we are familiar with one aspect of this tradition—the celebration of Mardi

Above right: Many of the déguisements *(dress-up costumes) celebrated regional or national costumes. This Bleuette 6/0 wears the* "Costume de Suissesse" *from patterns in issues #23-24, 1914 in* La Semaine de Suzette. *This example was created by Mathilde Hertier of Paris.*

Right: This brown-eyed SFBJ Paris 60 8/0 is wearing the "Costume d'alsacienne," *from patterns in issue #14, 1915 in the magazine. Mathilde Hertier stitched the costume, which is now in the collection of Suzanne Gautrot.*

Gras in New Orleans just before Lent begins.)

In another celebration, mid-Lent was a brief time to take a break from all the dietary and behavioral restrictions of this Holy Season. People might choose to dress up and act as they secretly wished they could. As mid-Lent approached, even the newspapers and special publications for children offered ever-more exciting and complex patterns for dress-up costumes. Adults and children alike joined in the fun and gentle naughtiness as they attempted to find ways to be "King for the day."

In the nineteenth century, just before Bleuette was "born," the new and increasing bourgeoisie gave parties and dances for children at this time of year. Since the purpose of these gala social events seems to have been to expose the parents' financial and social status, the parties often featured ostentatious displays of food, decorations, and luxurious clothing.

The elaborate dress-up costumes for children served as a link between two very different eras in children's dress. In the eighteenth and early nineteenth centuries, children were dressed in little replicas of adult clothing. No accommodation was made for a child's need to exercise developing limbs. The era of viewing the child as a miniature adult was succeeded, in the nineteenth century, by Jean-Jacques Rousseau's perception of children as young, unformed beings who needed to be protected, nurtured, guided and cherished for the potential they represented. As children were liberated by the changing attitudes of society, their clothing began to take on a much more age-appropriate style and construction. Styles in children's clothing began to evolve in the late nineteenth century, setting the stage for a real transformation in the design of children's clothing.

Bleuette enjoyed taking part in the mid-Lenten tradition.

Ruth Brown has costumed her 301 Bleuette to represent Bécassine as a very young child.

Marcene Oxford created this delightful "Folie" costume from the pattern in issue # 2, 1917. The points on the over-skirt and collar end with a colorful tiny bell, so appropriate for a jester's costume.

After the difficult and meager times during World War I, but before the deprivations of World War II, the French sought to recapture the enjoyment of social festivities, parties and dances. Bleuette's first dress-up outfit was printed as a pattern in *La Semaine de Suzette* in 1922. The first four patterns included a Peasant of Normandy dress, Pierette and Pierrot costumes and a Little Red Riding Hood (*Le Petit Chaperon Rouge*) ensemble.

The success of the first dress-up costumes encouraged the editors to produce sixteen more. Some of the patterns were only published once, but the more popular ones were repeated through the years. Also, some of the earlier costume patterns printed in *La Semaine de Suzette*, while not specifically designated as such, could be considered dress-up ensembles; *i.e.* costumes from other countries, nursing uniforms, some of the sporting outfits and the Bécassine costume.

The *déguisements* for Bleuette can be divided into several categories. The classic French costumes include Pierrette, Pierrot and Harlequin. Fairy tales were represented in fantasy costumes for Cinderella and Little Red Riding Hood. Foreign costumes included ensembles for: a Russian peasant; a Japanese lady; a Balkan peasant; a Mexican; and a Normandy farmer. A little Dutch girl costume came complete with wooden clogs. There was also an elaborate Swiss costume and a darling Scottish outfit, as well as traditional costumes of Italy; Germany; Serbia; Spain; Arabia; Persia; and Vietnam. In addition, costumes for various occupations were included, such as: nanny; nurse; dancer; pilot; tramway worker; sailor; and soldier. Obviously, the young owners of Bleuette were encouraged to learn about the world through creative play with their little doll.

TRUNKS, LUGGAGE AND BOXES

A steamer-style trunk was soon a necessity—what better way to store Bleuette's wardrobe? The first trunk for Bleuette was offered in the catalog of 1920.[40] It was called the *Rapide* and featured a tray, making two compartments for storing clothing and the doll. By 1928, a simplified trunk containing just one compartment was advertised. It was called "The Express." Collectors today have a difficult time identifying Bleuette's trunk. The blue paper-covered trunk with flat lid, leather strapping and metal protective corners was distributed by other

The Bécassine costume was certainly a fun way for little girls and their dolls to dress-up and play "Let's Pretend." This Première Bleuette, 1905, wears a Bècassine dress sold by Gautier-Languereau in 1916.

Perhaps one of the first lessons when one begins sewing with vintage fabric and original, historic patterns is that the colors are quite different from the hues we see today. This is particularly true in children's clothing. This "smart" little dress was made by Suzanne Gautrot from a pattern published in 1921. The slide-through belt and decorative blanket-stitching were used frequently in clothing during this decade.

An enduring decorative stitch for children's clothing is smocking. This simple frock from 1936 is modeled by a Unis France 251. The dress is called, simply, "Smocks."

vendors beside Gautier-Languereau.

A pattern for making a similar trunk was printed in *La Semaine de Suzette*, Issue 29, 1917. The pattern includes instructions for making the outer "box" of heavy pasteboard. Real wood strips are added on the outside to strengthen the trunk. The interior features a tray, which rests on narrow strips of wood/cardboard inside the trunk. The trunk could be painted, or the desired look could be achieved by gluing embossed paper on the outside and pretty printed paper on the inside of the trunk.

Patterns were also created for additional carrying cases that Bleuette needed for her various activities. Of course, she needed a small sewing basket, complete with lace-edged needle holder and a separate pincushion. Since Bleuette took various kinds of music lessons, she needed several music "rolls," all carefully embroidered, to carry her sheets of music. She needed a number of hatboxes in different sizes to contain her many hats. Bleuette had numerous *sac de voyage* cases for her shorter trips. Again, these were always beautifully embroidered. In 1909, a pattern for a *sac fourre-tout*, or carry-all, was given. The pattern for this rounded case offered a charming example of Bleuette's name to be embroidered on her case.

A group of Bleuettes is ready to go to town in Lille, France. Costumes include, left to right, "Côte Basque," Spring-Summer, 1928, catalog; a dress from 1926, made by the owner; "Crânement," Summer, 1932; "Tablier d'après-midi," 1905; and a knitted sweater shown in the Winter 1930 catalog as "Trés sport."

Bleuette also needed a wide variety of purses, some dainty and beaded, others larger and more tailored. There were patterns for making a wallet for protecting her small valuables. In the autumn of each year, patterns for schoolbook bags were published, in addition to patterns for the school uniforms and dresses.

FURNITURE

Some of the most innovative patterns in *La Semaine de Suzette* were for making furniture for Bleuette and for her dolls. In 1923, instructions for making two darling little baby beds, using household objects, were offered. One featured half a round box, covered with pretty fabric and supported on small wooden legs. The other was a simply made fabric-covered rectangular box, with an eyelet ruffle over-lap. The same crossed wooden legs were used; these looked like the supports for a standing sewing or knitting bag.

If a child could not afford to purchase furniture for Bleuette, an appropriate bed could be made from a sturdy cardboard box, "upholstered" in patterned fabric, with a mattress covered in the same fabric. The pattern in *La Semaine de Suzette* gave instructions to complete the bed with soft square cushions, made from the same fabric to form a back to the bed. The bed then became a divan during the day, and a bed at night. A simple knitting tool was created by placing four small nails in one end of a wooden thread spool. Using a winding, weaving technique, wool yarn could be "knit" into colorful tubes. When enough of these tubes were made, they could be carefully stitched together with buttonhole thread to form a small oval rug to place beside Bleuette's bed.

To complete Bleuette's little room setting, the reader was urged to gather old cigar boxes from her father and uncles. She could then paint them or cover them with pretty paper. Instructions were given for adding a mirror to the underside of the lid, and adding tape to the sides to keep the lid from falling over backwards. A second cigar box could be readily turned into a delightful bookcase, complete with a cabinet door. A pattern to make a dressing table from a cigar box included instructions for a tilting mirror made with the clever use of wooden spools.

Obviously, no sturdy items went to waste in the home where a Bleuette resided. Later, patterns were offered for a more modern, tailored couch, a cardboard armoire

This interesting pattern was first offered in the Gautier-Languereau magazine of Summer 1929. It was revised for the Spring-Summer catalog of 1952. Called "Fraîcheur," this example was made by Ruth Brown. Ruth made her collar as a separate piece, but the antique version of this dress has the collar as part of the dress. The doll is not a Bleuette; she is marked DEP and is of French manufacture.

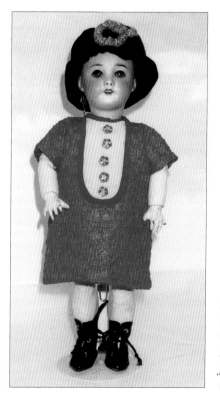

Bleuette 71 Unis France 149, 60 8/0, is all set to go to town wearing "Xenana" made by Suzanne Gautrot of Paris, from La Semaine de Suzette, *issue #29, Summer 1926.*

and a writing desk. Bleuette's mama could even make a small buffet cupboard to hold Bleuette's fine dishes. Various motifs were offered in the pages of *La Semaine de Suzette* to be traced onto the furniture and painted. Even the colors of paint were given. Some of the motifs featured stylized flowers. Nursery rhyme designs were also offered. In 1932, a motif for Little Red Riding Hood was given, complete with a windmill design. That same year, the design for a small lamp table featured an image of Cinderella, a large pumpkin and a clock striking midnight!

In 1906, the magazine presented patterns scaled for Bleuette's favorite doll, Mignonette. This little four-inch bebe was given to Bleuette for Christmas 1905 and became the focus of Bleuette's furniture-making experiences. The child mother practiced many skills as she cut out the furniture, colored it and glued the various pieces to sturdy cardboard. The resulting little furniture pieces were styled just like real furniture in the early 1900s. Later, when Suzette became the child "mother" to Bleuette, patterns were given in a much larger scale appropriate for Bleuette's use. Again, the furniture was in the very latest design of the time—first art nouveau, and later, art deco. Thus, not only was the trousseau of Bleuette always at the height of modern fashion, the furniture associated with her was equally inspired by the current designs in fashion.

Although the patterns provided hours of crafting fun for girls, Gautier-Languereau also realized girls might prefer to purchase already constructed furniture for their Bleuettes. In 1954, the spring catalog featured a very modern bed, complete with linens. In 1957, a bed and accessories were offered. A simple wooden clothes rack on which to hang dresses was depicted in the same catalog. Other furniture available for Bleuette included: tables and chairs; armoires; cupboards; lawn chairs; a basic canvas-sling beach chair; and a boldly striped beach house.

GAMES AND PASTIMES

All types of simple games were drawn or suggested in the pages of *La Semaine de Suzette*. Some of the games could be played by a girl alone; others were designed for group play. Many involved paper folding, similar to origami. There were even instructions for making paper floral bouquets, then creating an entire little flower shop. The necessary vases could be made from cans

[7]

In the 1930s, the use of contrasting binding to add interest and definition to costumes, became popular in the United States, as well. In 1931, the William E. Wright & Sons Company published a colorfully illustrated booklet with instructions on techniques for using their various tapes.

covered with pretty papers, according to instructions in the magazine.

The games also included jigsaw puzzles and word-picture matching games. There were rebus exercises, and "scientific" experiments to test hearing and seeing double with only one eye. These experiments required simple tools and paper. Another activity with paper was the creation of a color wheel.

Various directions and patterns were given over the years so that a child could create toys from easily found materials, such as nutshells or the shells of gum-nut balls. Patterns for very small furniture to be made of cardboard were presumably offered for Bleuette's doll, Mignonette.

In addition to porcelain-headed Mignonette, Bleuette also had a small black rag doll in 1918. Directions for making this little rag doll from cotton fabric were given in Issue 11, 1918. The finished doll was called Bambina or *Fleur de Blé Noir* (Flower of Black Wheat).[41]

A favorite indoor game offered in 1939 was a Bécassine ring toss set. The game pieces were made of cardboard and the colorful figures printed in *La Semaine de Suzette*. Additional games were specific to special holidays, like Christmas or Easter, or associated with important events, such as Baptism and First Communion.

Whether created from patterns or purchased ready-made from Gautier-Languereau, Bleuette's wardrobe and accessories permitted her to be dressed in the height of fashion for every activity a young girl could imagine. Always, the patterns and clothing for Bleuette were just what real little girls needed and wanted. There was a rich sense of practicality in the patterns, but also a delightful encouragement to seek adventure. Some of the patterns were for clothing that only very well-to-do little girls might have needed. But all little girls aspired to dress their dolls in the very best and latest fashions. In this process of discovery, girls were able to experience the joys of fashion, and what being in style really means.

This Bleuette SFBJ 301 is fortunate to wear this beautiful Christening robe from the Winter 1916-1917 Gautier-Languereau catalog. The ensemble includes a gown, an outer cape and a bonnet. The gown, measuring 10 ½ inches from shoulder to hem, is made of soft white cotton with cotton lace trim down the front, along the hemline, and mitered along the neckline and sleeve cuffs. The front panel features seven tiny tucks and two rows of lace insertion. It closes in back with a thread loop and small button. The gown was originally shown with a large white ribbon rosette attached to the front. The outer cape is made of heavier, woven white cotton with a ribbed design. The long body of the robe is sleeveless. A short capelet of the same woven cotton covers the upper arms and chest of the baby. Both the robe and capelet are outlined with a shiny, white feather stitching; the capelet is further trimmed with wide white lace. The bonnet is completely constructed of white cotton lace with a ruffle framing the face and neck. Originally, the bonnet had a ribbon rosette over each ear. The bonnet and cape are fastened with silk ribbons.

7

GAUTIER-LANGUEREAU'S WARDROBE FOR BLEUETTE

Real challenges confront the collector today who desires to own some of the exquisitely designed and stitched Gautier-Languereau clothing. Very few of the costumes were tagged. One must rely on a knowledge of fine fabrics, fineness of stitching, appropriately scaled buttons, closures and trim, as well as recognition of that indefinable bit of flair. The ready-made clothing shows beautifully finished seams on the interior of the garment. Much of the hand-stitching is so fine and even that it can easily be mistaken for machine work. The fabrics are rich in color and texture. Depending on the decade, designs have a definite Art Deco or Art Nouveau aspect. The collector needs to begin her search, armed with knowledge of the look and feel of quality, vintage fabrics. A close study of the catalogs published by Gautier-Languereau shows what specific styles to look for. With the exception of the war years when some costumes were never produced in the fabrics that were protrayed in the catalogs, the collector/researcher can gain much knowledge by studying the catalog drawings and descriptions.

Before catalogs were available, some clothing, hats, lingerie and shoes were offered in advertisements printed in *La Semaine de Suzette*, under the heading: *"Le Trousseau de Bleuette."* These advertisements must have been success-

Several nursing costumes for Bleuette were offered in the Gautier-Languereau catalogs. There were also patterns for nursing uniforms in La Semaine de Suzette, such as this one, called "Les Metiers de Bleuette," which appeared in #45, 1929, worn by an SFBJ 301.

A brown-eyed 6/0 sits for her picture in
"Garçonnet," (little boy) from La Semaine de
Suzette, *#15, 1910. She wears calf-high leather boots*
made by a child. This ready-to-wear costume, in a
dark-red fabric, was advertised in La Semaine de
Suzette, *#26, 1912.*

ful in spite of their lack of color and limited graphics, because they soon led to the publication twice a year of catalogs that featured charming drawings of each costume advertised. Until 1916, the patterns in *La Semaine de Suzette* were the same as those used by skilled seamstresses hired by the firm of Gautier-Languereau to produce ready-made clothing for Bleuette, but with the advent of the Winter 1916-1917 catalog, the patterns in the magazine were different than the patterns used for costumes sold through the catalog.

The firm of Gautier-Languereau was virtually synonymous with the printing of fine children's literature in France. Thus, they used their excellent resources to hire outstanding artists who drew the fashions advertised in the catalogs. Maggie Salcedo and Manon Lessel were just two of the artists who brought the clothing into visual form through their artistic skill.

Beginning in the winter of 1916, a small catalog advertising ready-made clothing to fit Bleuette was published. The first page of this premiere catalog featured the drawing of a young girl holding the hands of her small doll on a table. The title of a short article on this page was *"Bleuette, La Poupée qui suit la Mode, et son Trousseau."* (Bleuette, the doll who is up-to-date in fashion, and her Wardrobe). Little girls who did not yet own a Bleuette could purchase one for 4.75 F. Of course, there was also an advertisement for *La Semaine de Suzette.* Although non-illustrated advertisements and patterns for a wardrobe were published in the magazine from the very beginning, this small catalog was the first opportunity little girls had to purchase quality, ready-made clothing created just like the images they could see in the catalogs. The venture was an instant success, and the catalogs continued to be printed twice a year until the end of Bleuette's production (with a brief interruption during World War II).

This first catalog set the tone for all the future offerings. Each costume had an imaginative name that evoked a sense of adventure and romance. The child was encouraged to see Bleuette as a girl of spirit, action, and adventure, always dressed in the very latest, fully accessorized fashions.

A beautiful taffeta coat in dark blue, along with a blue velour hat, garnished with lavender Louis XVI ribbon, which was sold separately, was featured in the first

catalog. On the same page, a blue serge skirt with open pleats was offered. The chemisette was made of fine white wool cloth, and had a lavender ribbon bow at the neck. The following page featured two very popular garments for Bleuette that are often found today. One is the rather military-looking coat called *Joffre* in blue, with red embroidery and a matching peaked hat. The ensemble was completed by leg gaiters, which were made of supple leather to fit the legs well.

The other costume on this page was the ever-popular nursing outfit of a Red Cross worker, fittingly titled *Croix-Rouge*. The ensemble included a dress, an apron with Red Cross emblem and a head covering—all of which were white—

Bleuette wears three different ensembles on this page from the Winter 1930-31 catalog drawn by Maggie Salcedo. Note the different hairstyles and hemlines on these little "girls."

From left: "Blanchette," was featured in the Winter 1922-23 catalog. "Sophie," is from the Summer 1924 catalog. "At Home" was shown in the Winter 1924-25 catalog. These costumes were on display in 2000 at the special Bleuette Exhibition at the Musée de la Poupée in Paris.

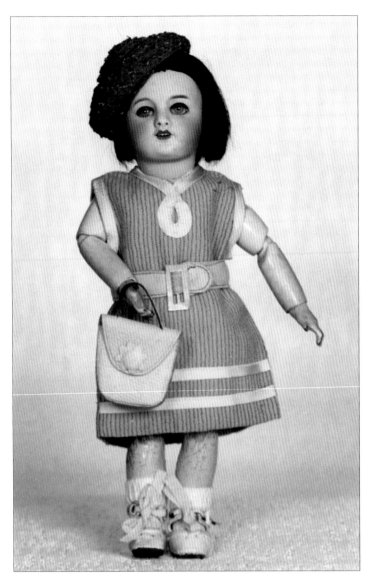

Bleuette SFBJ 60 8/0 looks très chic *in "Fantasie," made with dark chartreuse wool with gold-edged white silk trim, Summer 1931. Her hat, shoes, stockings and purse were all made and sold by the firm of Gautier-Languereau.*

and a deep-blue cape, which also had a red cross appliquéd onto a white square on the left front side of the cape. Bleuette was also ready to come to the aid of France in a naval costume (which remained very popular throughout Bleuette's production) and "Tipperary," a costume based on an English military uniform.

In the center of the catalog are four costumes that illustrate well the wide variety of influences in Bleuette's outfits. The center pages have hats, coats and dresses in exotic styles evoking Russia and the Philippines. The style of Brittany is portrayed by the Bécassine-style costume.

The catalog continues with pages of charming dresses, coats and hats for every occasion. Shoes, boots and gaiters were also offered. One page showcased only hats—each appropriate for completing the other costumes sold in the catalog. Finally, essentials such as exquisite lingerie were offered. Included were corsets; stockings; panties; chemises; a taffeta under-skirt; linen handkerchiefs with dainty lace edging; and an elegant

This Bleuette 6/0 welcomes spring in her very chic coat, hat and dress ensemble from 1935. The coat is "Tartare," from the Gautier-Languereau Spring 1950 catalog. Her jaunty hat is the "Chapeau Breton" from Spring 1952, while the pink print dress is one of the many variations of the costume "Smocks."

apron in nainsook, trimmed with entre-deux and satin ribbon. The grand costume on one page is a long, elaborate Baptismal gown and bonnet, with a beautifully embellished double cape to complete the ensemble. Although we think of Bleuette as a young girl, each catalog continued to offer clothing appropriate for an infant, such as: nightgowns; dresses; coats and bonnets; aprons; and corsets, as well as corset covers. Bibs were offered repeatedly, as were patterns to make additional ones. Knitted and crocheted clothing, ranging from dresses to capes to sweaters and scarves were also pictured in the catalogs. Obviously, Bleuette could be costumed for whatever age her young mother wished.

Just this brief overview of the first catalog suggests why these small fourteen-page booklets are avidly sought-after by collectors today. Anyone interested in following the changes in doll costuming over a forty-four-year period can find this information in these catalogs. Likewise, since Bleuette's wardrobe was always at the forefront of high fashion for young girls, the cata-

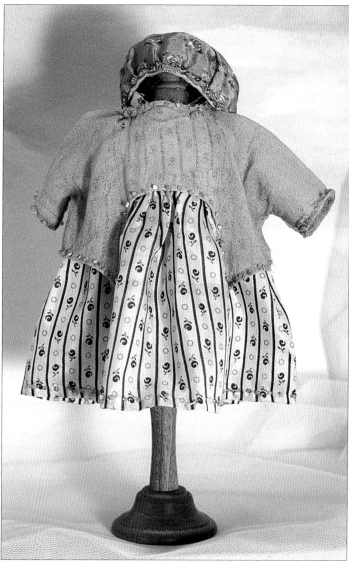

"Stella" is a two-piece ensemble featured in the Gautier-Languereau Spring-Summer catalog of 1919. The skirt and bodice for the dress is flowered surah. The over-blouse is of fine silk crepe, edged with seed pearls to accent the interesting contour of the lower edge of the top. The outfit was completed with a "toque Stella" hat in silk file with accents of seed pearls. The entire ensemble sold for 8.50 Francs.

Recognizing authentic Bleuette costumes sold by Gautier-Languereau takes a bit of detective work. Obviously, clever seamstresses can duplicate costumes based on images in the catalogs. The buyer should examine the garment carefully, paying attention to small details. In this pastel version of "Smocks," worn by a Bleuette 6/0, the blue chain-stitching at the yoke and bordering the smocking is precisely lined up. The smocking is created with pink thread in exact rows of stitches. The bodice is lined. The hem on the sleeves and skirt are machine-stitched. The dress closes with a small hook and thread loop, and the back opening is beautifully hand-finished.

logs provide a rich source of visual information on fabrics, colors, trims, as well as styles and types of clothing considered appropriate for girls between 1916-1960.

In an early discussion of Bleuette's trousseau in one catalog, a list of necessary items was offered to help girls know just what their dolls needed for the coming summer. Included were hats of straw, embellished with fanciful trims of gauze, flowers, frills of silk, and ribbon. Or, the young lady could purchase unadorned hats and trim them herself. This catalog went on to suggest a number of ensembles including: a mariner's costume; a town dress; a traveling coat; a dress in velvet cloth; a fancy lace and silk dress; a woolen dress; a bathing dress in flannel with linen shoes and a bathing hat; several coats and capes; and a Bécassine costume with dress, silk apron, bonnet, veil and cloth shoes.

Of course, Bleuette also needed lingerie. The first item is an under-robe of nainsook and lace, called a "Jackson." Then she needed day gowns and nightgowns; slippers; pantalons; petticoats; underpants; a corset; bibs; collars; a school apron; a dressier apron of nainsook; a peignoir; and a dressing gown. Although these items were offered for sale in the catalog, similar items could be made from patterns in *La Semaine de Suzette*. The magazines recommended the items in the catalog, and the importance of subscribing to the magazine was mentioned in the catalogs. Both publications also advertised other products sold by the firm of Gautier-Languereau, such as books about Bécassine and dolls made in her likeness.

Above left: Few composition-head 301s are preserved as well as this cheerful child. She is all dressed for the city in her wool suit, called "Lavandou," from Winter 1938-39.

Left: Every little girl loves her puppy, and Bleuette is no different. Bleuette, composition head 60 8/0, is wearing the lovely knitted coat called, "Spahl," from Winter 1939-40. Her puppy is made of blue vinyl-like fabric. He is shown in an advertisement from the pages of La Semaine de Suzette, *1939. In the advertisement, he is wearing a doggie jacket with a big "B" on it. He also came with a leash. The puppy was named "Ric" and came in blue, red or white; he cost 12.50 Francs.*

During the first years Gautier-Languereau offered ready-made clothing through mail order or direct purchase from their offices. These clothes were much the same as the garments made from patterns published in *La Semaine de Suzette*. But with the advent of the printed catalog, the clothing presented was exclusive to the catalogs. Patterns in *La Semaine de Suzette* were different. The catalogs featured high-fashion clothing of entirely original design, always in the latest colors and fabrics, echoing the styles for adult ladies of the day.

Manon Iessel also drew for the pages of *La Semaine de Suzette*, and even created a comic strip about Bleuette in every issue from 1950-1960.

If we examine the catalogs by decade, certain trends become obvious. In her first decade, Bleuette was dressed in delicate draped dresses with silk ribbon and beautiful lace trim. There were instructions for creating *broderie anglaise*, which was then used on dresses, collars and cuffs, and lingerie. These costumes were quite detailed, both as patterns and in the catalogs. In fact, the patterns may have proved so challenging that they began to be simplified in 1916, as the catalogs continued to offer the more complex fashion designs. The early years of Bleuette's production coincide with the end of the Victorian period, and the start of the Edwardian Era. Ladies and girls wore some of the most delicately feminine styles possible, with beautiful lace and tucking, and soft, flowing lines.

Then, as the year 1920 approached, Bleuette's dresses

Above right: Clever use of inexpensive wool felt allows for colorful costumes with a minimum of sewing. These jackets by Ruth Brown were fashioned after the "Armor" jacket in the Winter 1956-57 catalog.

Right: Lest anyone get the wrong impression, while Bleuette was used as a teaching tool, she was also meant to inspire enthusiasm for sewing. This post-World War II 301 is wearing the result of one little "mother's" enthusiasm—what she lacked in skill, she made up for with sheer determination. The coat features covered buttons, a set-in collar and a very free-form hemline! Bleuette also wears old stockings and leather shoes made by Mathilde Hertier of Paris.

The high-fashion design elements on Bleuette's clothing could be quite simple. This Bleuette 301 is wearing the elegant "Citadin" wool coat and hat from the Winter 1923-24 catalog. In this costume, the influence of Paul Poiret is seen in the svelte silhouette and contrasting color trim, which adds a sense of movement to the coat. The use of colorful contrasting binding in dresses, coats, jackets, even pajamas, adds a liveliness to the costumes.

become shorter. The waistline continued to be ill-defined. The creative genius of innovative *haute-couture* designers in France began to appear in costume designs for Bleuette. The strong influence of Paul Poiret and his School of Decorative Art, Martine, was seen in Bleuette's costumes, which were also influenced by such artists as André Marty. Marty may also have drawn some of the designs in the Spring-Summer catalog of 1919, as suggested by the signature on one of the pages. But the images in the next catalog, Winter of 1919-1920, were drawn by an artist who signed herself Colette.

By 1921, Bleuette's dresses and skirts were shorter, usually showing her detailed knees. Plaid fabrics and pleats were used frequently. Her wardrobe included many coats, capes, raincoats and jackets to keep her comfortable in all kinds of weather. In each collection of costumes, there were also carefully designed hats. Obviously, a well-dressed young French girl needed a stylish *chapeau* to complete each ensemble. In these early catalogs, Bleuette was frequently drawn with soft curls that fell to her shoulders. Even if her hair was shown in a wavy bob, she was often depicted with a large bow in her hair.

But in the Winter 1922-23 catalog, Bleuette was shown with a very modish straight bob haircut, slick and stylized. The fabric of her clothing now had strongly figured prints and geometric, influenced by the clothing of fashion designer, Paul Poiret. The artist chosen to draw Bleuette's new look was M.M. Baratin. It is interesting to note that Bleuette was rarely shown sitting demurely or just standing around. Instead, she seemed to be always on the go and busy with activities: putting her dolls to bed; jumping rope; riding her scooter; chatting with friends—this very modern young lady was occupied with many happy pursuits.

Paul Poiret was deeply affected by the painting and room decoration styles created by the School of Martine, which he founded. These organic, complex textile designs were used in the most fashionable clothing, as well as in avant-garde interior design and furnishings. The prints had bold lines, strong colors, a sense of liveliness and movement. Many suggested a very strong Oriental influence. Similar prints, in greatly reduced size, were incorporated into Bleuette's garments in that same era.[42] Another fashion designer

This dress also shows the strong influence of Poiret in the almost-organic look of the print fabric, the sharply contrasting trim and use of colorful buttons to accent design elements. This dress is similar to dresses and fabrics shown during the Exposition of the Grand-Palais in Paris, in 1924. Sadly, this delightful costume was produced in prototype only; it was never offered in the catalog.

The influence of fashion designer Elsa Schiaparelli is seen in this ensemble from Summer 1931, called "Domino." The costume shows the injection of color that was a signature innovation of this great designer. The tailoring is very precise, creating a lively, sophisticated look for Bleuette, 71 Unis France 149, 301.

whose styles found their way into Bleuette's wardrobe in the 1920s was Coco Chanel. These strong textile patterns may have suggested the need for a simpler line to clothing.

In the Spring-Summer catalog of 1926, there was a surprise: a small advertisement for Bleuette's newly arrived baby sister, Benjamine. Benjamine was drawn wearing a pique dress and bonnet trimmed with embroidery. In a second image, she was shown in a crocheted romper with stripes in red or blue. The graphics depicting Benjamine were repeated in advertising in *La Semaine de Suzette* in 1926, as well. Since Benjamine enjoyed a very brief exposure, this was her only mention in the catalogs.

The next time a younger member of Bleuette's family would be mentioned was in the Summer of 1929, when sweet baby clothes for Bambino were added to the catalog. After Bambino was introduced in 1928, Issue 43 of *La Semaine de Suzette*, new additions for his

Suzanne Gautrot of Paris created this bright ensemble. The dress and vest are from "Ensemble fleuri" (floral ensemble) offered in La Semaine de Suzette, *#24, 1929. The purse is from the pattern, "Sac a ouvrage pour Bleuette" (Work bag for Bleuette).*

wardrobe were shown in the Gautier-Languereau catalogs of Bleuette's clothing. In Summer, 1929, Bambino had an entire page of fashions, which included a Christening gown, robe, bonnet and knitted romper. The doll himself was offered dressed in a knitted wool and silk romper, with booties, and a knitted cap that tied under his chin. He sold for 58 francs. Bleuette was shown seated beside Bambino in a new embroidered jacket. Soon, Bambino's wardrobe covered several pages in each catalog. A Christening gown was offered regularly. There were usually various knitted costumes as well, for outdoor activities and playtime at home.

Much has been written about the influence of Madame Languereau, wife of Henri Gautier's nephew, on the fashions of Bleuette. Madame Languereau was friends with Madame Jeanne Lanvin, the celebrated *haute couturière*, who was known for designing stylish children's clothing as well as high-fashion apparel for adults.

In the 1930s, Bleuette's classic "Marine" costume changed. Instead of a loose over-blouse, the costume, now called "Costume Marine Classique," featured a tucked-in blouse and skirt-band with two prominent buttons for trim. The béret *is embroidered with the word: "Maginot" on the hat band. The costume is from the Winter 1933-34 catalog.*

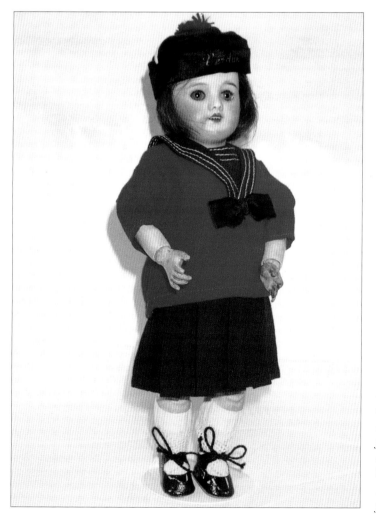

As in each era, there were several "Marine" costumes for Bleuette in the 1920s. This 71 Unis France 149, 60, 8/0 wears "Marine Bi-colore" from the Winter 1923-24 catalog. This lively red and navy combination, with the pom-pom topped béret *proved so popular that it was offered again in 1926. The costume was produced in wool serge and jersey, too.*

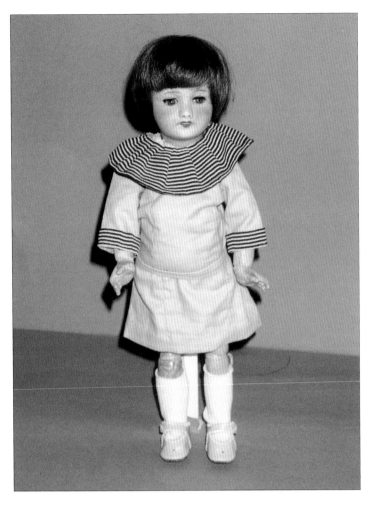

However, there is no firm evidence that Lanvin ever actually designed for Bleuette, even though her stylish influence was definitely the inspiration behind many of Bleuette's ensembles. In all likelihood, seamstresses who worked for the high-fashion houses also stitched the small Bleuette costumes in order to make extra money. It would also seem natural that Madame Languereau would intuitively incorporate design elements from her friend's work into the designs for Bleuette. In addition, she sought inspiration from other designers, including the incorporation of bias-cut styling made famous by Madeleine Vionnet. (Vionnet was also known for her use of small mannequins, or dolls, to display her creations and for working out fashion details.) In the Summer 1930 catalog, the costumes presented were called "particularly elegant." Some of the costumes from Gautier-Languereau and patterns in *La Semaine de Suzette* were inspired by the styles created by Wiener Werkstatte, which were much in vogue in the 1930s.[43]

By the mid-1930s, innovations such as the plastic zipper were finding their way into the world of fashion. Although zippers were first introduced in 1912, they were infrequently used until the mid-1930s, when a better locking mechanism made them practical. Zippers were not generally used in doll clothing, but when the famed designer Elsa Schiaparelli introduced the concept of letting the zipper show as a design element for garments in 1935, they soon appeared in Bleuette's clothing as well. The Gautier-Languereau catalog for Winter 1935-36 featured a darling ski outfit, *Sur Les Cimes*, with a wide zipper closure prominent

Above left: This dress with the ruffled collar and matching trim on the three-quarter-length sleeves is apparently a copy of the dress "Junior," which was featured in the Winter 1936-1937 catalog. The model is a 71 Unis France 149 301 1 ¼. She wears a replaced wig, shoes and socks.

Left: The lovely light turquoise "Estival" ensemble included a skirt, blouse and jacket with clever detailing and buttons on the lapels.

It is tea time for the Bleuette girls all dressed in their "Marine" costumes. This nautical theme was a traditional part of Bleuette's wardrobe from 1905 to 1960. The happy tea table is set in the home of Suzanne Gautrot. The dates for the costumes, from left are: Winter 1933; Summer 1925; Summer 1934; Winter 1960; and Winter 1926. Variations of the costume were published in every Gautier-Languereau catalog, as well as in pattern format in La Semaine de Suzette.

Right: All little girls seem to love an excuse to get all dressed up. Bleuette, 71 Unis France 149, 301, is wearing "Cérémonie" from the Winter 1933-34 catalog.

Left: Although the mascot doll for the magazine, Lisette, was larger than Bleuette, this Unis France 301 Bleuette seems quite happy to wear her frock made from a pattern in Lisette. The skillful use of the geometric border-print fabric recalls the clever use of fabric design in the 1920s and 1930s. Bleuette is holding her favorite puppet, made by contemporary doll artist Faith Wick.

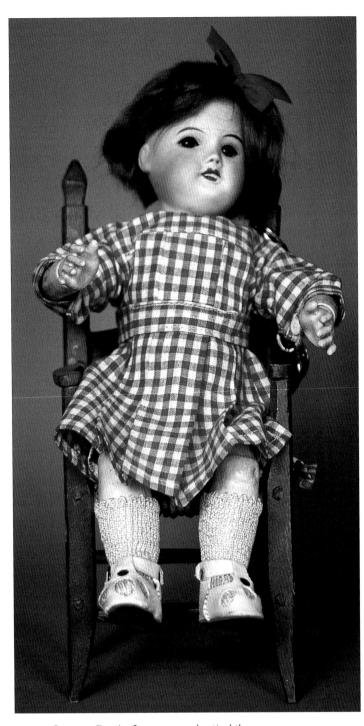

In 1930, Gautier-Languereau advertised the charming red-and-white checked "L'Enfant sage" (wise child) in La Semaine de Suzette. *The half-page advertisement depicted Bleuette wearing various costumes. The drawings surround a "box" containing the Gautier-Languereau motto: "La Poupée est la Reine des Jouets. Bleuette est la Reine des Poupées." (The Doll is the Queen of Toys. Bleuette is the Queen of the Dolls.) Bleuette 60 8/0 is wearing sandals (kneip) with her school apron. This is the first model of Bleuette made after World War I. She has painted as well as real eyelashes framing her pretty sleep eyes.*

on the front of the garment. The catalog description compared the garment to an aviator's uniform. In fact, as World War II approached, the influence of military styling was noticeable in each catalog.

Schiaparelli's whimsical approach to fashion design also influenced Bleuette's wardrobe. Her touch of fantasy and imagination is apparent in the treatment of sleeves, as well as over-sized button trims, and the innovative use of standard trims, such as fringe and rickrack.

World War I was the impetus behind the increase in production of ready-to-wear clothing by Gautier-Languereau, which in turn led to the publication of the twice-a-year catalogs. Many believe that the period between the two world wars, after 1918 and before 1939, was truly the Golden Age of Bleuette.[44] Fortunately, World War I did not deter little girls from continuing to costume their Bleuettes in fine styles. Shoes, dresses, hats, lingerie, and all the other necessities for dolls continued to be sold by Gautier-Languereau during and after the war.

Somehow, the "magicians" at Gautier-Languereau managed to keep up production with ever-new designs in fabric and clothing. However, this was not to be the case during World War II, when life under the German occupation of Paris became very difficult for all the French people.

Gautier-Languereau Publishing was told by the Germans to cease publication of *La Semaine de Suzette.* For a time, they were permitted to sell back stock from their store on rue Jacob. When the magazine was stopped, the publisher had to rely on the sporadically published catalogs to sell his stock. Paper was in short supply for all manner of items. Little girls were urged to bring bags and boxes with them to the shop. Soon, Gautier-Languereau had to warn their young customers that the fabrics featured in the catalogs might have to be replaced. Procurement of fabric became a great problem.[45] The last catalog to follow the familiar format was the Spring-Summer issue of 1940. There was a quarter-page advertisement in 1941-42, which stated *"Voici le Catalogue Hiver 1941-1942."* (Here is the catalog for Winter 1941-1942.)

For four years, there was no printed word about Bleuette, but the Gautier-Languereau store somehow managed to keep its doors open, continuing to sell its back stock. New ensembles from this time period are

very rare, and difficult to document. Recent research by Suzanne Gautrot of Paris has confirmed some of the clothing from this period.[46]

Finally, in May 1946, publication of *La Semaine de Suzette* resumed. In a series of charming advertisements, Bleuette was re-introduced, along with a complete wardrobe. The publication noted that she is "as beautiful as before the war years, always dressed tastefully according to current means."[47] Bleuette was accompanied by other familiar faces—those of Bambino and Bécassine.

Nicole Ward Jouve has written a touching evocation of the deprivation of the French people during the war years and immediately afterwards. It is notable for its reference to *La Semaine de Suzette* and Bleuette.

My father said, 'I am going to take you to the cinema tonight to see The Gold Rush.' I did not know what 'cinema' was. It was one of those wonderful and unimaginable pleasures, like La Semaine de Suzette, *and its doll Bleuette, which the war had taken away. Grown-ups would evoke them discreetly, so as not to make you envious, not to corrupt you with impossible desires. They would say, 'Before the war, there was......' My grandmother had a beautiful satin box with flowers painted on the cover. She hoarded ribbons in it. She said, 'You see, before the war, this was given to me as a present, and it was full of chocolates.' I could not imagine what they were, apart from an unattainable marvel, part of a world gone forever.*[48]

After World War II, Bleuette was sold completely dressed for the first time. Previously, she had been sold only in varying designs of a simple chemise. In August

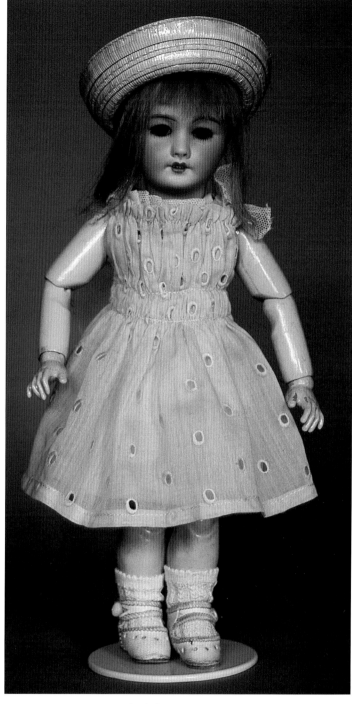

This lucky Unis France 301 is wearing a lovely springtime dress, "Vingt-neuf a L'ombre," from the Spring-Summer 1938 catalog.

Can anyone doubt that these five little Bleuettes are enjoying a festive costume party? The Bleuettes were part of a display in Lille, France, in the early 1990s.

This lovely plaid taffeta dress is complete, except for a white hankie in the pocket on the left breast. It was introduced in the Winter 1954-55 catalog, and remained part of the catalog until 1960. The dress was priced at 375 francs, plus shipping.

1946, Bleuette had a multi-pieced First Communion costume, including a smocked dress. However, by November, Gautier-Languereau had to announce the temporary halt of selling Bleuette until they could build up their stock again. From November 1946 through 1947, there was no mention of Bleuette in *La Semaine de Suzette*. Finally, in the first half of 1948, new costumes began to be available for Bleuette. But there were still no catalogs. The paper shortage continued to be a problem in France.

Preceding the return of the actual catalogs, however, there were large advertisements in the newly revived *La Semaine de Suzette*. The first catalog after World War II, published in Winter 1950-1951, featured the delightful draftsmanship of Manon Lessel. The catalog showed a very active Bleuette in animated conversation with friends, running in the wind, attempting to ski and playing with Bambino. Bambino was depicted with a decided "baby face" with chubby cheeks and a soft expression. Obviously, Bleuette had a renewed zest for life—and she needed a great many outfits for her varied activities: swimming suits and cover-ups; tennis dresses; a Scouting costume; outerwear for all types of weather; party dresses; lingerie and nightclothes; and the ever-popular First Communion gown.

This very popular dress was featured in the catalogs of 1950-51. "Croquiquolette" shows what a careful choice in rickrack and buttons can do to spice up a simple blue dress. This dress is made in navy-blue cotton in the Gautier-Languereau catalogs. This example was made by Ruth Brown from vintage cotton and trim.

Bambino also had new outfits for all his activities: play clothes; bibs; nightclothes; dress-up shirts and short pants; rompers; and Christening dresses. Bécassine was reintroduced, and Gautier-Languereau also advertised a Clinic for Dolls, complete with a drawing of Bleuette and Bambino swathed in bandages.

By 1952-53, Bleuette had such thoroughly modern clothing items as slacks and sweatshirts. A delightful line of small suitcases made in plaid fabrics was offered for Bleuette's travels. She now had long ceremonial gowns in her wardrobe, too.

In the Spring-Summer catalog of 1955, Bleuette's older sister was introduced. Although she would become known as Rosette, she was introduced in the catalog as a 35-centimeter Bleuette. She came with either a porcelain head or a composition head. She had sleep eyes and a fully articulated body. Nine costumes were listed for the 35-centimeter doll, as well as shoes and stockings. They were the same as the Bleuette

Left and below: "Garden Party" from the Spring-Summer 1953 catalog is worn by a Bleuette 301 at left, and shown as part of a display at the Musée de la Poupée in Paris, below. The same dress was also available with the print in green.

The dress "Silhouette" was very popular in various colors. The dress was featured in the Winter 1954-55 catalog. A variation also appeared in issue # 30, 1953, of the magazine.

costumes, except in a larger size.

Rosette's name was first used in the Winter 1955-56 catalog; an expanded list of outfits was available for her. In a charming drawing in Spring-Summer 1956, Rosette was shown in a plaid dress and her hair was styled in pigtails. She was called Bleuette's older sister in this catalog. Bleuette soon added such accessories as a sleeping bag and tent. Her sports gear increased. A bed with linens was offered. Bleuette took up sailing and needed new outfits suitable for this pastime, too. In Spring of 1958, Bleuette was shown using her lovely clothes rack as an exercise pole! She added croquet to her costume needs, and was then shown helping her "mother" by vacuuming the floor.

In the Winter 1959-1960 catalog, Bleuette, Rosette, Bleuette 58 and Bambino were all pictured. The Bleuette 58 was 33 centimeters (13 inches) tall. She was

Below: "Printemps Jolie" (beautiful springtime) is epitomized by this pink silk coat, from the Printemps catalog 1952. The pocket detail gives an added dimension to the silhouette of this coat, which was perfect for spring evenings.

Below right: As Bleuette came to the close of her long career, her creators at the firm of Gautier-Languereau continued to show delightful costumes and patterns in their magazines. In 1950, this coat with the wonderful detailing on the front was offered in the catalog. This version of "Comfortable," including the tassled tam, was sewn by Ruth Brown.

manufactured by the Gégé firm, which gave rise to her name. The head is marked with the name, "Gégé" and so Bleuette 58 is often called Gégé. She is jointed at the neck, shoulders and hips. The Bleuette 58 is difficult to find today since she was produced for only two years. Separate costumes were offered for each doll. Bleuette and Bleuette 58's outfits were identical, although the prices were different. Rosette had her own separate list of costumes, and of course Bambino had whole pages devoted to his wardrobe.

Sadly, this was to be the final catalog. The directors of Gautier-Languereau announced that their stocks were completely exhausted. The long production of Bleuette and the publication of *La Semaine de Suzette* ceased, bringing to a close a glorious era. At that moment, who could have imagined that a day would come when Bleuette would once again be the sought-after little princess of French Fashion?

In Winter 1952-53, the "Slalom" set of slacks and a sweater was very popular. These two Unis France 301 dolls were sold at the Galeries de Chartres, Chartres, France in 1999. The dolls are sitting on the Scots plaid suitcases offered in the catalogs in the 1950s. Ensembles with trousers were now accepted in France, at least for sporting activities. Girls still wore dresses or skirts and tops, however, for most of their activities.

CHAPTER

8

Patterns to Make by Louise Hedrick

No book about Bleuette would be complete without patterns. Today, a new group of enthusiasts is becoming acquainted with Bleuette and the tradition of creating a fashionable wardrobe for the doll, using hand-sewing techniques and appropriate fabrics.

One of the most outstanding and beloved teachers of heirloom sewing today is Louise Hedrick of Elm Grove, Wisconsin. Louise has brought her passion for sewing details to the world of collecting through her membership in the United Federation of Doll Clubs and the Doll Artisan Guild. She has taught and lectured extensively on heirloom sewing and the appropriate costuming of antique dolls. In 1999, Louise discovered Bleuette. She began an in-depth study of the early patterns and appropriate fabrics for executing them, while examing the techniques taught in *La Semaine de Suzette.* She recognized that the invitation to sew implicit in Bleuette's history is part of the doll's allure for collectors, many of who have never sewn a stitch. In an effort to encourage more collectors to discover the joys of handsewing, Louise has created a series of patterns inspired by those published in *La Semaine de Suzette*; five of these are presented on the following pages. Readers are invited to enter the realm of Bleuette and her wardrobe with Louise Hedrick as teacher and guide.

FIVE PATTERNS FOR BLEUETTE: 1906-1933

The enchanting clothing patterns from *Nous Habillons Bleuette* inspired little girls during the entire Bleuette history. Five patterns, each representing the period of their models-the first five generations of Bleuette, are presented in this chapter. These patterns were originally published not only for the little girls' enjoyment of their dolls, but to teach them the important sewing disciplines of the day. Thriftiness was also promoted; little girls were encouraged to use what they found in Mother's sewing basket, rather than to purchase expensive fabrics and laces. Patterns for the earlier dolls were more complicated than those that appeared later, but all the patterns throughout the first thirty years of Bleuette's history depended greatly on the use of fine sewing and embroidering techniques. I have included directions and diagrams for some of the most commonly used techniques below.

This clothing was meant to be hand sewn, but machine sewing can easily be substituted. **In all instances a 1/4" seam is assumed and included in the pattern.** Although all of the Bleuette bodies look almost alike, both the antiques and reproductions have small variations in the body parts, such as diameter of the arms, chest, etc. Therefore, it is most helpful to make a muslin sample of the pattern before cutting into good fabric. It is also a good practice to have the doll wearing her undergarments when fitting a dress. Some fabrics fray a great deal, so get in the habit of sealing seams with Fray Check or similar product.

The patterns, each modeled by a doll from the appropriate period, are presented on the following pages.

• Page 142: The Première Jumeau Bleuette wears a sleeveless Mariner's dress with matching jacket and beret from *La Semaine de Suzette*, #31-33, 1906. (This ensemble is also worn by the doll on the cover of this book.)
• Page 148: The 6/0 model wears a simple summer dress from *La Semaine de Suzette*, #4, 1915.
• Page 152: The SFBJ 60 model wears a scalloped embroidered full slip and matching drawers made of fine Swiss batiste from *La Semaine de Suzette*, #12 and #50, 1919.
• Page 156: The 27-centimeter 301 wears a Christening ensemble from *La Semaine de Suzette*, #48-49, 1928.
• Page 160: The 29-centimeter 301 wears a robe from *La Semaine de Suzette*, # 49, 1932, and pajamas from *La Semaine de Suzette*, #11, 1933.

HEIRLOOM SEWING TECHNIQUES

The following are the simplest of the hand-sewn heirloom techniques that were used on these garments.

• **French seam**
  1: Place wrong sides together, stitch 1/8" seam, press to one side, trim as close to the stitching as possible.
  2: Place right sides together, stitch another seam 1/8", making certain you have covered the first seam.

• **Rolling and whipping (Mock)**
  If you are not familiar with the traditional method, this one is easy to learn and accomplishes the same thing.
  1. Working from the wrong side of the fabric, fold top edge of the fabric toward you 1/16".
  2. Work from right to left. Hide the knot of your thread under the fold and take a tiny stitch in the top edge of the fold.
  3. Take the next tiny stitch just off the fold into the main piece of the fabric and a little forward. Your needle will pierce only the main piece of the fabric, not the folded-over portion.
  4. Repeat for an inch or so. The effect will be zig-zag stitches. Draw thread up and the hem will roll. Repeat to the end of the project. See diagram below.

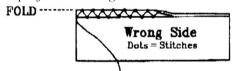

• **Attaching lace to a rolled edge**
Lace can be applied straight or gathered. To apply lace straight, work from the right side, with the fabric and lace side by side, not overlapping. The stitch is a whip stitch, going into the very bottom of the roll of the fabric, and then into the heading of the lace. If you have to go around a corner, gather the lace so that the outside edge will lie flat.

To apply gathered lace, measure the length of the rolled edge. Cut the lace 1-1/2" times the length. Pull the heaviest thread in the heading of the lace to gather it to fit the rolled edge, distribute gathers evenly and whip on as described above.

• **Stitching diagrams:** The following diagrams appeared in *Nous Habillons Bleuette* to explain scallop stitches, buttonholes and feather stitching: there was no written information.

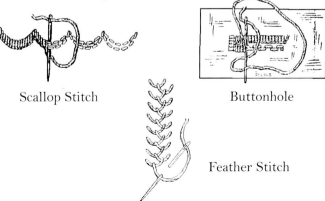

Scallop Stitch   Buttonhole

Feather Stitch

Mariner's Ensemble

MATERIALS

- 1/4 yard wool challis, other light-weight wool or firm cotton
- 1/8 yard cotton for lining
- 3 yards soutache braid in contrasting color
- DMC to match soutache
- 1/3 yard ½" satin ribbon to match soutache
- 4 size #1 hooks/eyes
- needle and matching threads

Options: The decorative brass anchors (3) and brass clasp were obtained from "Cat's Paw," which is listed under suppliers in this book. An alternative to the brass anchors would be to hand-embroider anchors in the same places. An anchor design is shown at the end of these directions. A closure on the jacket could be made with 2 tiny brass buttons connected with a thread loop. Anchor one end of the loop over one of the buttons and sew down.

Dress Construction: Cut front, two backs, skirt, lining, neck bias piece and two sleeve bias pieces. With right sides together stitch the bottom edge of the skirt to the bottom edge of the lining. Turn lining to wrong side and steam press well. Pleat skirt in 3/8" pleats all around. Steam well and let dry throughly. Pull lining away from skirt to open up completely, sew center back seam leaving open 1-1/4" at the top. Then put lining back in place. Press under opening seam allowances and blind stitch. Add three rows of soutache braid beginning 1/4" up from the bottom of the skirt. Leave a space of 1/8" between each row. Stitch the soutache with a running stitch down the center of the braid in the ditch.

Sew shoulder seams of bodice and overcast. Fold in seam allowance of the back as shown on the pattern and press. Blind stitch. Stitch bias, right sides together to armhole, turn to wrong side leaving 1/4" of bias showing on right side. Turn raw edge under and blind stitch. Stitch side seams and overcast. Stitch neck bias in the same manner as the armhole.

With right sides together, stitch skirt to bodice, easing in fullness where necessary. Close the back with three hooks on one side, the first at the neck, the second at the waist, and the third half way between. Stitch thread loops on the other side. Stitch brass anchor at the neck at center front, or embroider an anchor in the same place.

Jacket Construction: Cut one back, two fronts, two sleeves, one collar, one collar lining, and bias strip. Sew shoulder seams and overcast. Stitch sleeve dart, including slashed area. Hem bottom of each cuff. Sew two rows of soutache braid to the bottom of the cuffs as you did on the skirt. Stitch sleeve seams.

MARINER'S ENSEMBLE

Gather top of sleeve as indicated on pattern and pull up gathers to fit in armhole. With right sides together, stitch and overcast this seam.

With right sides together, stitch along the outer edges of the collar, turn and press well. Stitch two rows of soutache braid as you did on skirt all along the outer edges of the collar. Pin the raw neck edges of the collar to the jacket. Begin at center back and work toward the front, easing as you go. Repeat with the other side. The collar should stop at the solid fold line of the pattern. Stitch with the right side of the bias against the right side of the collar. Turn the bias to the wrong side, turn under raw edge and blind stitch. Hem the bottom of the jacket. Turn in seam allowance of jacket fronts, first 1/8", then 1/4", then press and blind stitch.

Two brass or embroidered anchors should be placed in the corners of the collar in back. The jacket is closed with a hook and thread loop on the inside, and a clasp on the outside.

Beret Construction: Cut beret top, bottom and band. With right sides of the top and the bottom together, stitch around that circle. Turn. Steam press this seam as sharp, round and flat as possible.

Prepare band. The original pattern suggests that the name of a ship be embroidered on the brim. This can be done by hand or machine. Some suggestions were: l'Etoile, l'Esperance, and la Belle-Poule if you wished a feminine name. Maritime bird suggestions were la Mouette, l'Abatros, and le Goeland. Position the embroidery so that the center of the name is at center front and on the top half. Hem the short ends of the band. Press. With the top of the band, right side, against the right side of the bottom of the hat, stitch. Turn the band to the inside, turn under the raw edge, and blind stitch. Steam press the band into a sharp edge at the bottom. Cut two pieces of satin ribbon, each 1 inch long. Stitch just to the left of the name on the brim. This will be to the side. Then make a "cocarde" or rosette to stitch over the raw edges as follows:

Cut a piece of satin ribbon 5" long. Follow the diagram on the next page and stitch. Start 1/4" from beginning and end 1/4" from end. It is helpful to use a wash-away marker to mark the ½" points on your ribbon. Leave your needle threaded when you get to the end. Thread another needle and hem short ends. Pull up as tight as

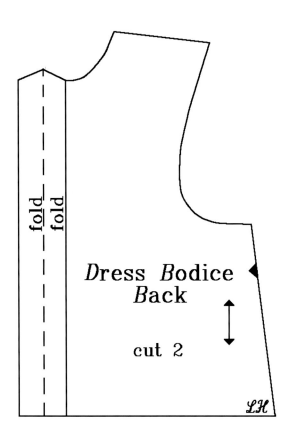

fold
fold

Dress Bodice Back

cut 2

𝓛𝓗

MARINER'S DRESS, JACKET AND BERET

Straight Pieces: Skirt: $3 - 3/4"$ x $25\frac{1}{2}"$, cut 1 dress fabric, 1 lining
                     Hat Band: $1 - 1/4"$ x $8\ 1/8"$

Bias Pieces: $2 - (1"$ x $2\frac{1}{2}")$ dress fabric for dress sleeves
                     $3/4"$ x $4\frac{3}{4}"$ lining

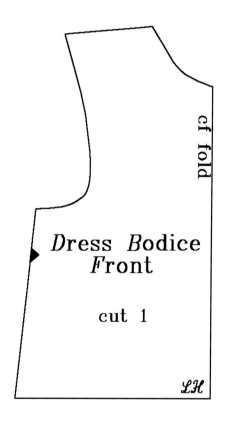

Dress Bodice
Front

cut 1

cf fold

𝓛𝓗

1/4"   ←1/2"→   1/4"

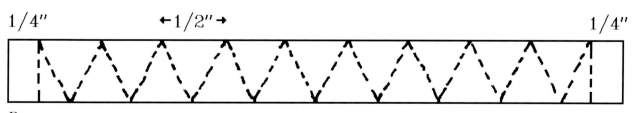

Rosette

possible to form the rosette. With needle and thread go through each point of the rosette on the inner circle. Whip back and forth to secure. Without cutting the thread, stitch the rosette to the raw edges of the streamers on the headband.

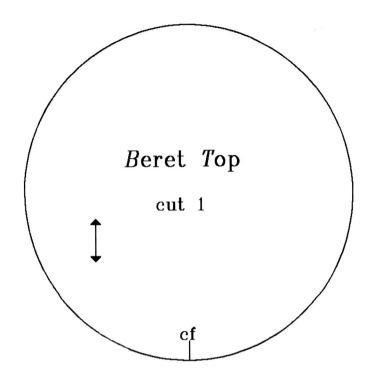

Beret Top

cut 1

cf

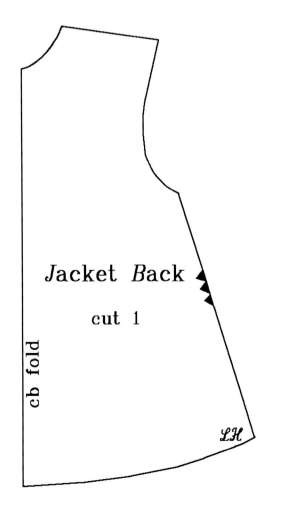

Jacket Back

cut 1

cb fold

LH

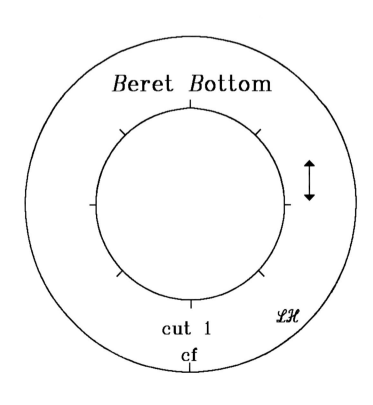

Beret Bottom

cut 1

cf

LH

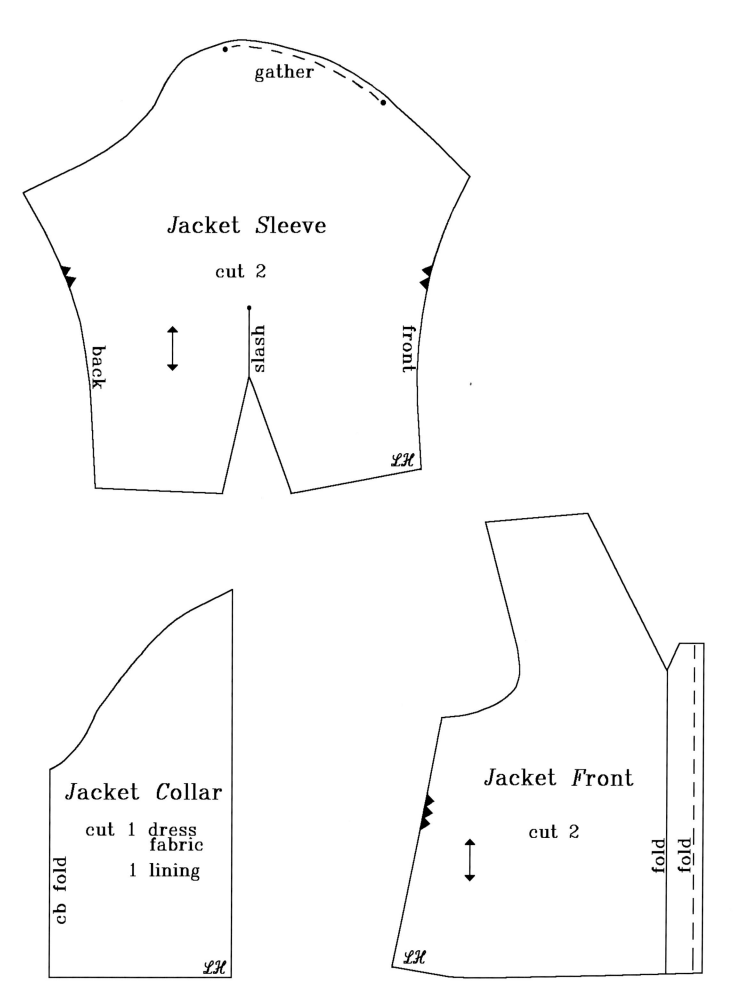

Jacket Sleeve

cut 2

gather

back

slash

front

LH

Jacket Collar

cut 1 dress
fabric

1 lining

cb fold

LH

Jacket Front

cut 2

fold

fold

LH

SUMMER DRESS

MATERIALS

- 1/4 yard lightweight cotton
- 3/4 yard ½" silk satin ribbon to match or contrast dress
- #30 embroidery thread for machine embroidery
  or
- DMC embroidery floss, one package
- 4 size #1 hooks/eyes
- needle and hand-sewing thread

Options: The original dress was designed to give the sewer experience in practicing her embroidered scallops and buttonholes on the skirt, bertha, sleeves and belt. There are wonderful scalloping and buttonhole patterns available with today's computerized sewing machines. You might also choose to make the dress white and use purchased Swiss cotton embroidered edging, 2-3/4" wide and purchased beading that is 1" wide. If you do this you need only a small piece of regular white batiste, 1-1/4 yards of edging and 1/3 yard beading. The edging would have to be trimmed for the bertha and sleeves.

Dress Construction: Cut one front, two backs, two sleeves, skirt, bertha, belt and bias piece. Construct skirt, bertha, sleeves and belt by whatever option you choose from above.

Fold center back seam allowance under and blind stitch. French seam shoulder and side seams of bodice. French seam sleeves, gather to fit armholes and stitch. Overcast these seams. Gather the neck edge with two rows of gathering threads, following the guide on the pattern. Place on the doll to determine fit. Gather bertha to fit neck edge and stitch to neck. With right sides together, stitch bias to neck over bertha. Turn bias to the inside, turn raw edge under and blind stitch.

Turn short ends of belt in 1/8" twice and blind stitch. Gather bottom edge of bodice to fit the belt and stitch on. Overcast this seam and press up. French seam skirt seam leaving open one inch at the top. Turn under seam allowance of opening and blind stitch. Gather top of skirt to fit the belt, stitch this on and overcast. Close the dress with one hook at the top, the second 1-1/2" down, the third and fourth at the top and bottom of the belt. Stitch thread loops on the other side.

Cut a piece of satin ribbon 9 inches long and thread through the button holes. Turn raw edges under and fasten on wrong side. Tie a single or double bow with the rest of the ribbon, leaving streamers long, and sew off center on one side of the belt.

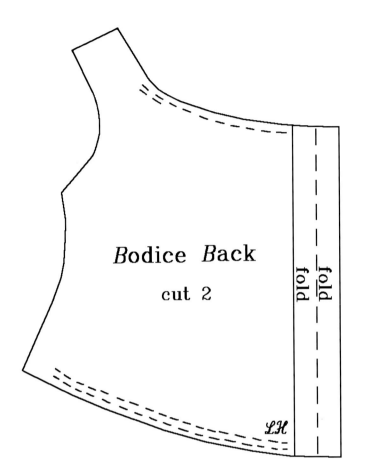

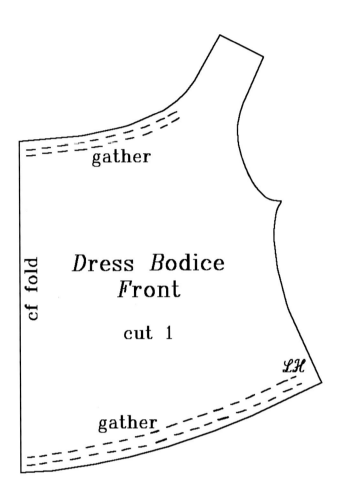

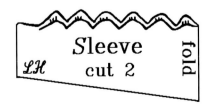

SUMMER DRESS

Straight Pieces: Skirt: 2¾" x 16"
                    Bertha: 1¾" x 18"

Bias Piece: Neck: 3/4" x 6½"

Skirt Width Pattern

2¾" x 16"

Bertha Width Pattern

1¾" x 18"

Belt — cut 1

Slip and Drawers

MATERIALS

- 1/4 yard Swiss batiste or fine cotton

- White size 30 machine embroidery thread
  or

- DMC embroidery floss

- ½ yard 1/8" white tape

- Two tiny two-hole pearl buttons

- needle and thread

- See options

Options: The original pattern was designed to have hand-sewn scalloped ruffles on the drawers and slip. The neckline and armholes repeated the same scallops. The work could also be done on a sewing machine. A further option is to roll and whip the neckline and armholes and finish with 1/4" lace (½ yard) whipped onto the edge. The petticoat ruffle and drawer legs could be finished with purchased 1-1/2" Swiss embroidered edging, the edging on the drawers trimmed to 3/4", 1-1/4 yard required.

Another use of this pattern for the slip that was popular in France at this time was to make this as an "under dress," which is the literal translation of "robe dessous." The slip was made in a pastel color to be worn under a sheer white dress. The neck, armholes and ruffle were trimmed with a very narrow simple lace, tatting, or crochet edging.

Slip Construction: Cut out slip front, two sides and two backs. If you are doing scallops by hand or machine, draw on scallop design with washout pen, but leave extra fabric beyond the scallops. If you will hem and attach lace, draw line from tip of scallop to tip of scallop, cutting along this line. Then roll and whip this edge when the slip pieces are together. Stitch sides to front, then to backs easing the fabric as you go.

Turn in seam allowance of the back as shown on the fold lines of the pattern, press and blind stitch. Cross these folded edges at the bottom and stay stitch a couple of stitches to hold. French seam shoulder seams. Cut ruffle and hand or machine scallop at this time and trim, or use purchased embroidery. French seam ruffle, gather the top to fit the lower edge of the slip and with right sides together, stitch. Overcast this seam and press up. Feather stitch just above this seam, catching it as you sew to hold it flat. Sew two buttons to close, one at neck and one 1-1/2" below. Stitch worked button holes to match on the other side.

Drawers Construction: Cut back, front and belt. Construct two pieces of scalloped ruffle 3/4" x 7" by whatever method you used for slip. French seam side seams. Seam waistband; this seam will be at center back. Make two worked buttonholes 1/4" on either side of the center back seam. They should each be 1/4" in

SLIP AND DRAWERS

length, started 1/4" from the bottom of the fabric. When the waistband is finished, they will be at center back on the inside. With right sides together stitch waistband to body, seam at center back. Turn to inside, turn raw edge under 1/4" and blind stitch.

Gather leg ruffle to fit leg opening. With right sides together stitch, overcast seam and press up. Feather stitch just above this seam, catching it to hold it flat. String 1/8" tape from buttonhole to buttonhole around the waist.

Straight Pieces:
slip ruffle: 1¾" x 16"
drawers waist band: 1" x 8½"
drawers ruffle: 2 – (3/4" x 6½")

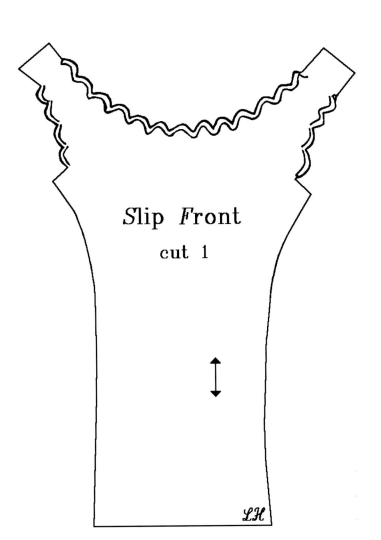

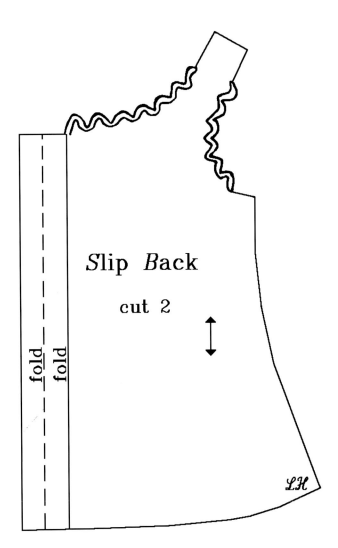

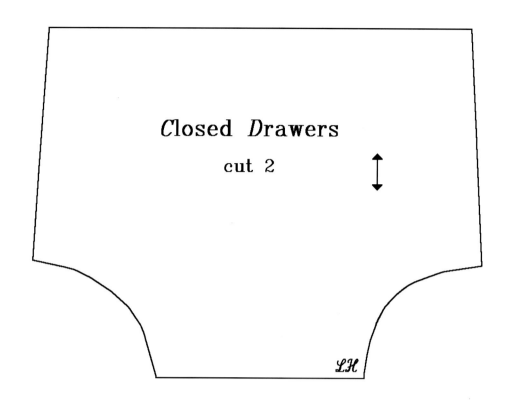

Closed Drawers

cut 2

LH

Slip Ruffle Template

$1\frac{3}{4}''$ x 16"

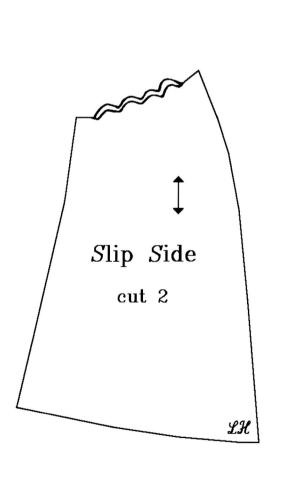

Slip Side

cut 2

LH

CHRISTENING ENSEMBLE

MATERIALS

DRESS AND SLIP

- ½ yard white batiste or fine cotton

- 1-1/2 yards 5/8" insertion lace

- 1 yard 1" edging lace

- 1 yard 1-3/4" Swiss embroidered edging

- ½ yard 1/4" edging lace

- Four tiny two-hole pearl buttons

- needle and matching thread

CAPE AND BONNET

- sheer silk, (such as silk batiste), ecru, 9" x 26" for cape fabric

- ecru cotton flannel or wool challis, 9" x 26" for cape lining

- 1-3/8 yards 1-3/4" Alencon or heavier lace edging

- ½ yard 1/4" ecru silk satin ribbon

- 2/3 yard ½" ecru silk satin ribbon

- 12" seam binding

- ½ yard 1/8" white tape

- matching thread

Options: The original skirt of the christening dress shows three rows of 5/8" insertion lace stitched 3-1/4", 4-3/4", and 6-1/4" from the top of the skirt. There is also a row on edging lace stitched to the bottom of the skirt. Suggestions for this are: Do all stitching by machine, using the pin stitch, or pin stitch all by hand. If you do one of the above, the fabric can be carefully cut from behind the lace. The third option is to stitch by hand the insertion lace at these intervals and leave the fabric in place. Then roll and whip the bottom edge and whip the edging lace to this rolled edge. If you use this third method, French seam the center back seam before applying the edging lace.

Slip Construction: Cut skirt, front bodice, and two back bodices. French seam shoulder seams. Roll and whip neck edge after folding in seam allowances at center back and pressing. Whip 1/4" lace edging to the neck edge. Roll and whip armholes and whip on same lace to each. Roll and whip the bottom edge of the skirt. Trim one side of the entredeux and whip this to skirt. Trim other side of entredeux. Trim 17" of embroidery to 3/4", roll and whip the top edge and whip onto lower edge of entredeux. Repeat with 1-3/4" embroidery. The narrower embroidery rests on top of the wide embroidery. If you wish, you could pin them together, treat as one piece, and do this in one stage.

French seam center back seam, leaving open 2" at the top. Turn under seam allowance of opening and blind stitch. Gather top edge to fit the bottom of the bodice. Stitch with right sides together and overcast. Press seam allowance up. Close the back with a button at the neck and at the bottom of the bodice. Stitch thread loops on the other side.

Dress Construction: Cut skirt, dress front, two backs and bias neck piece. French seam shoulder seams. Turn in seam allowance at center back according to pattern and press. Cut 8" of the 1" edging lace. Gather heading thread to fit neck edge and whip on. With right sides together, stitch bias neck piece over lace. Turn to wrong side, turn raw edge under and blind stitch.

Clip line between side seam and sleeve to dot. Turn sleeve opening under twice, press and blind stitch. Trim your 1" edging lace to 5/8" (4" for each sleeve) and

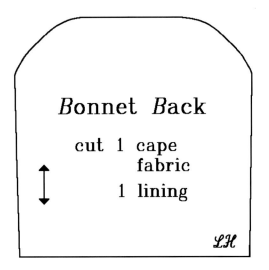

Bonnet Back

cut 1 cape
fabric

1 lining

LH

Slip Bodice Front

cf fold

cut 1

LH

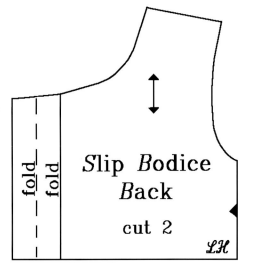

fold
fold

Slip Bodice Back

cut 2

LH

stitch to edge with a running stitch. French seam tiny side seams.

Complete your skirt by one of the methods suggested in "Options." Complete the skirt as you did the slip above. Close the back with a button at the neck and one at the bottom of the bodice. Stitch worked buttonholes on the other side.

Bonnet Construction: Cut two backs, front lining, and bias piece. Cut a piece of 1-3/4" lace, 6-1/2" long. Place wrong sides of the backs together and baste across middle to hold. With right sides together stitch the lace to the entire curved edge of the back. Remove basting. Roll and whip both long edges of the front lining. Stitch lining to cover the raw edge of the lace/back with a running stitch. Smooth the lining across the lace and with a running stitch secure this to the lace. The lace will extend from lining about ½". Take bias piece and turn under short ends and press. Turn under one long side and press. With right sides together, stitch across entire raw edge at the bottom of the bonnet. Turn bias to inside and press. Stitch other edge of bias. This forms a casing. Fasten two 9" pieces of tape to the outer edges of the bonnet. Draw up to fit the back of the doll's head and tie in a bow. Trim ends of tape. Attach 1/4" satin ribbon to front edges.

Cape Construction: Cut two main cape and two yoke pieces. Center cape lining over silk, top edges even and wrong sides together. A seam allowance will extend from each side and bottom. Press these toward inside and blind hem. Put the wrong sides of the yoke pieces together, centering the flannel on the top and sides, bottom edges even. Press seam allowances of neck and short fronts of silk to wrong side and blind hem. Gather top edge of body to fit, stitch and overcast yoke. Stitch seam binding over the raw edge. Cut 18" piece of 1-3/4" lace and stitch to bottom of the cape with a running stitch. Cut a 23" piece of the same lace, gather to fit the bottom edge of the yoke and whip on. Cut two pieces of ½" satin ribbon, 12" each and attach to either side of the neck. This, when tied in a bow, is the only closing.

CHRISTENING DRESS, SLIP, CAPE, AND BONNET

Straight Pieces:	Slip Skirt:	7" x 17"
	Dress Skirt:	8¾" x 17"
	Cape Body:	9½" x 17½"
	Cape Lining:	9¼" x 17"
	Bonnet Front Lining:	1¾" x 6¼"
Bias Piece:	3/4" x 5" for dress neck	
	3/4" x 6" cape fabric for bonnet back edging	

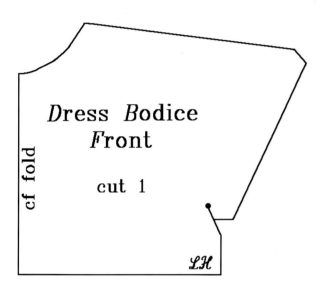

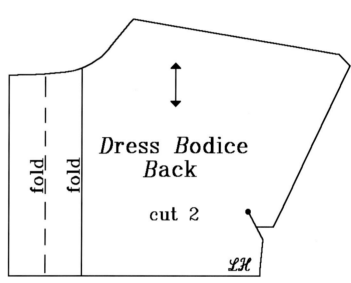

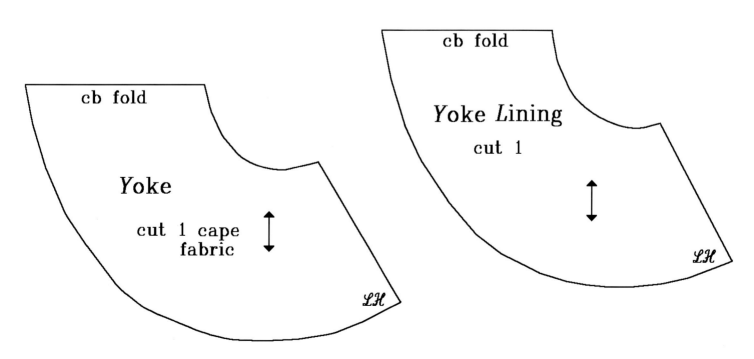

PAJAMAS AND ROBE

MATERIALS

PAJAMAS

- Medium-weight cotton: 9" x 22"
- Contrast fabric of same weight: 9" x 12"
- ½ yard 1/4" silk ribbon
- 6" narrow soft elastic
- needle and thread

ROBE

- 1/4 yard cotton flannel
- 30 weight machine embroidery thread or DMC hand embroidery floss
- DMC embroidery floss, l package for belt
- hand-sewing thread

Options: Pajamas can be solid or print. They should be 100% cotton. The scalloped collar and cuffs of the robe can be hand or machine embroidered. They could also be made by cutting them double with no scallops. With right sides together stitch on the outer edge, turn, press, and treat as other collar and cuffs. This set of patterns was made to fit the 29-centimeter Bleuette. Should you wish to adapt this for the 27-centimeter doll, shorten the pajama bottoms and robe by 3/4" at the bottom of each.

Pajamas Construction: Cut two bottoms, one front, and one back. Using contrast fabric, cut the seven strips. French seam center front and center back seams of bottoms. Stitch contrast fabric across the bottom of the legs with a 1/4" seam. Stitch under leg seam and overcast. Turn contrast fabric to the wrong side leaving a band of 1/4" on the top, turn under raw edge 1/4" twice, and blind stitch. Turn top edge under 1/8" and press, turn again 1/4" and press. Stitch this casing with a running stitch leaving open ½" at center back. Measure doll's waist, subtract 1/4", insert elastic and sew ends together. Stitch last ½" closed.

Stitch shoulder seams of pajama tops and overcast. Slash center front to dot, fold back and blind stitch. Stitch bias contrast fabric to neckline and both armholes. Finish as you did the bottom of the legs. Repeat with straight strips at the bottom of the tops. Stitch side seams before stitching contrast fabric to the wrong sides. Cut two pieces of silk ribbon and attach to either side of the neck. Tie in bow after it is on the doll.

Robe Construction: Cut back, two fronts and two sleeves. Prepare collar and cuffs by one of the three methods explained in "Options." Stitch shoulder seams, side seams and overcast. Stitch sleeve seams and turn sleeves to the right side. Stitch 1/4" cuff extensions. Place the right side of the cuff against the wrong side of the sleeve, with the seam of the cuff lined up with the outside of the sleeve. Stitch the cuff to the sleeve and overcast. Turn the cuff to the right side and steam press. Tack the cuff to the sleeve with a couple of stitches to hold in place. Gather the top of the sleeve to fit the armhole. With right sides together, stitch sleeve and overcast. Hem bottom edge. Find the middle of the collar, pin to robe with the right side of the collar

PAJAMAS CONTRAST FABRIC

Straight Pieces: pajama bottom: 2 – (1" x 5")

                     pajama top: 2 – (1" x 5")
                     contrast fabric

Bias Pieces: pajama neck: 1" x 7"
                     pajama armhole: 2 – (1" x 7")

against the wrong side and inside of the robe, stitch and overcast. Turn the collar to the outside and steam press so that it rolls softly. Stitch carriers at waist level in the side seams.

Construct the belt. Cut one full package (8 yards) of embroidery floss into six equal pieces. Place all six strands side by side. Tie ends to door handle and hang scissors in the middle. Holding the six strands in one hand, stretch tight and twist in one direction until you can't twist anymore. Hold scissors in one hand and bring all twelve ends together. Drop scissors and let cord spin until it stops. Cut ends from the knob. Tie these ends in a knot. Cut thread off scissors at the other end and tie those ends in a knot. Trim ends below knots. String belt through the carriers.

Bath Robe Front

cut 2

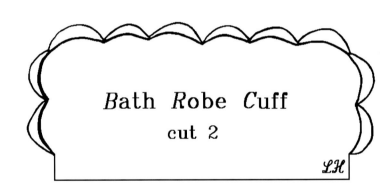

Bath Robe Cuff

cut 2

LH

fold
back
*

fold

Pajama Top Front

cut 1

LH

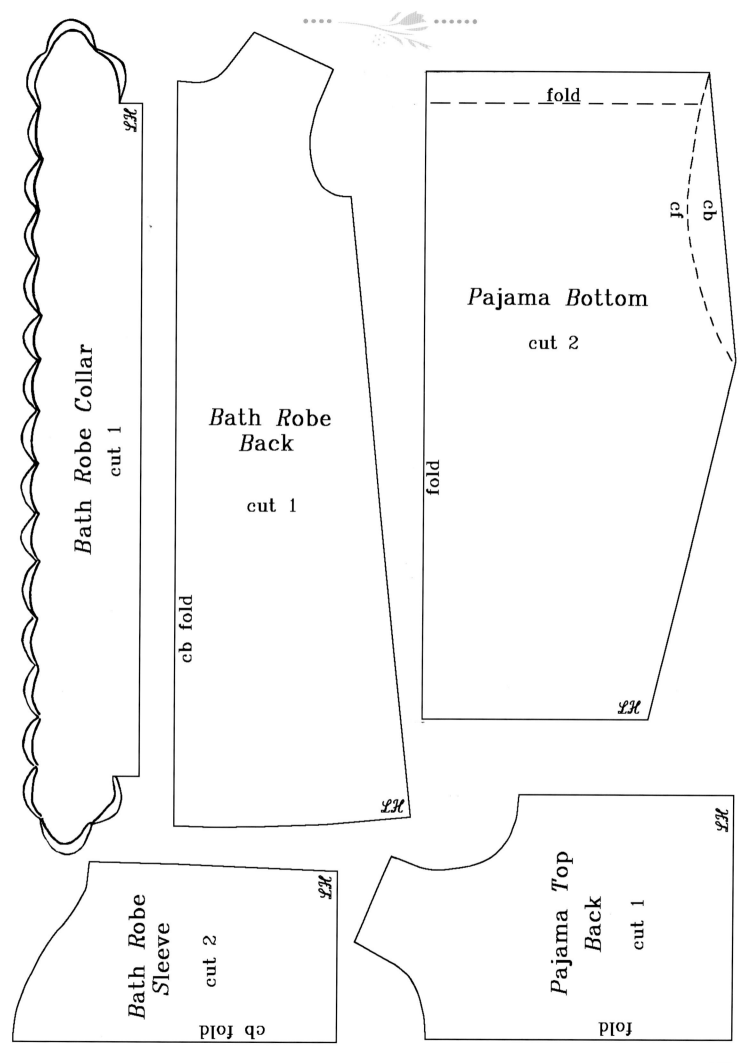

Bath Robe Collar
cut 1

Bath Robe
Back

cut 1

cb fold

Pajama Bottom

cut 2

fold

fold

cb
cf

Bath Robe
Sleeve

cut 2

cb fold

Pajama Top
Back

cut 1

fold

PART III REFERENCE

The items shown on these pages are described on page 175.

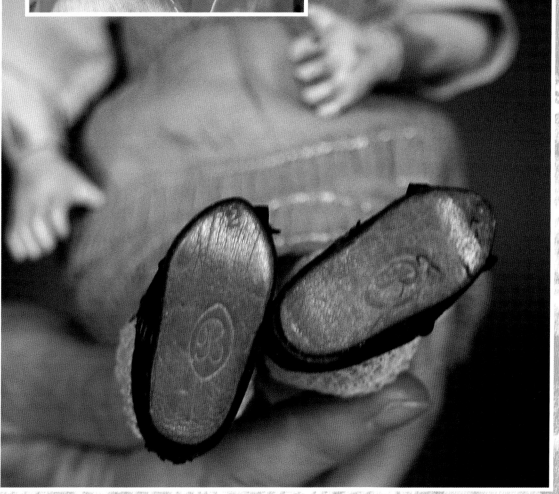

APPENDIX A
Markings

The markings on the back of a Bleuette's head are essential for attempting to identify a doll's authenticity and dates of production. Likewise, finding the marks on the body and feet can help ascertain that the body is that of a Bleuette. As noted in Chapter 4, markings can be missing or barely visible. However, the complete absence of markings is very rare. More often, a doll is found with the markings obscured by paint or by a wig, or as a result of the head being made from an over-used mold.

"Reading" the mold markings is rather simple, once the basic order of the information is understood. This information includes the country or city of manufacture, the number of the mold and the size of the doll. It might also include the initials of the individual dollmaker or the last two digits of the year of manufacture. For example, a typical marking might be:

23 (Year of manufacture)

SFBJ (Mark of the manufacturer)

60 (Mold number)

PARIS (Place of manufacture)

8/0 (Size of this model)

Here is another typical example, with the explanation following below:

71 UNIS 149

FRANCE 301

1-1/4

The number on the left in the first line is that of the National Union of Trade Syndicates. The number on the right in the first line was given by the *Chambre Syndicale* to its members. The UNIS FRANCE guarantees that the doll is entirely of French origin. 301 is the number of the mold. The final mark on the neck—1-1/4—gives the size of the doll.

The mark, UNIS FRANCE, was only used by SFBJ after 1924.[49] The UNIS in this mark stands for the *Union Nationale Syndicale*, which was a collective of various manufacturers sponsored by the *Chambre Syndicale*. The *Union Nationale* was founded in Paris in 1915 to market and protect products made in France.

The paper sticker sometimes found on Bleuette bodies was another effort to promote French products against foreign competition. SFBJ used this round sticker, in the French flag colors of red, white, and blue, before and during World War I.

A lucky Unis France 301 models her homemade dress featuring a deep-brown velvet bodice, and a skirt made of lengths of woven silk ribbon. The drop-waist style was very popular from 1923 through 1930 in the catalogs and in patterns.

APPENDIX B
Awards and Accolades

Throughout this century, Bleuette and her promoters were the recipients of many honors. Gautier-Languereau received the first award for excellence, a silver medal for Bleuette, in 1925, at the end of the Decorative Arts Exhibition, at which the Toy Village was featured. In 1931, Bleuette received the *Diplôme d'honneur* at the Colonial Exposition, even though Gautier-Languereau introduced the little black Bamboula during this event. In 1933, Bleuette was awarded a gold medal at the International Exposition of the Doll in Lyon. In 1937, she was awarded another gold medal at the Universal Exposition of the Arts. Finally, in 1985, Bleuette was featured on a bronze medal created by Mireille Lafrançois for the Ministry of Currency and Medals. The Première Bleuette is at the center of the medal, with a Steiner doll on her left and a Barbie on her right. The medal thus shows a timeline of dolls from 1885 to 1960.[50]

Of course, little girls did not need the affirmation of medals and awards to know that Bleuette was a very special doll. Even before Gautier-Languereau announced in 1929 in *La Semaine de Suzette* that: "The doll is the queen of toys, and Bleuette is the queen of the dolls," Bleuette's young owners had made her queen of their hearts. The accolades and enthusiastic acceptance of Bleuette led almost immediately to a rash of imitators. Gautier-Languereau finally copyrighted the name Bleuette in 1935, but the production of look-a-like Bleuettes continued.

Bleuette was also popular outside of France. She is mentioned in numerous books throughout the years, in a rather matter-of-fact manner suggesting that owning a Bleuette was a cherished memory of childhood. The English author, H.C. Cradock wrote in *Josephine and her Dolls*, in 1918, that Josephine said, "*Bleuette is my biggest child. She is very pretty and has nothing broken—except for one of her eyes, which is slightly damaged and doesn't close like the other one when you lay her on her back...........Her hair is curly and dark brown like her eyes. She bends everywhere, even at the knees and elbows..........This is handy when it comes to putting on her dresses and coats. She has a sweet character.*"[51] It was even said that the little English princesses, Elizabeth and Margaret, subscribed to *La Semaine de Suzette*, translating its pages and making doll clothes for Bleuette as a way of putting their French lessons to practical use. Perhaps an enterprising nanny recognized the universal appeal of the magazine for young girls everywhere.

This Bleuette, marked SFBJ 60 8/0, is wearing pajamas called "Bonne Nuit." The white pique nightclothes are decorated with red embroidery stitches. The pajamas also came with blue embroidered trim. The costume was shown in the catalogs for Bambino, as well as Bleuette, beginning in Winter 1924–1925, and continuing through the mid–1930s.

NOTES

PART I: THE DOLL

Chapter 1

1 François Theimer, *Madame La Poupée Bleuette*, trans. Paul Antal (Paris; Les Editions de l' Amateur, 1990), p. 8

2 Anne-Marie Porot et al., *S.F.B.J., Captivating Character Children* (Cumberland, MD: Hobby House Press, 1986), p. 4

3 Theimer, *Madame La Poupée Bleuette*, p. 6

4 Ibid.

5 "The Educational Value of Dolls," *Pedagogical Survey*, Dec. 1909, p. 9

Chapter 2

6 F. Theimer, *La Poupée Modèle*, Vol. I (Paris: Editions Polichinelle, 1997), p. 9

7 Marie-Anne Couderc, *Bécassine Inconnue* (Paris: CNRS Editions, 2000) p. 14

8 Hélène Bugat-Pujol, "Through '*Tante Jacqueline*'" (*L'univers de Suzette*, www.poupendol.com, 12-12-01). p. 4

9 Ibid.

10 Couderc, op.cit. p. 19

11 Miriam Formanek-Brunell, *Made to Play Dolls: The Commercialization of American Girlhood, 1830-1930*, (New Haven: Yale University Press, 1993), p. 124

Chapter 3

12 Hélène Bugat-Pujol, "A Bleuette Without Ambiguity," (*L'univers de Suzette*, www.poupendol.com, 8-14-2001), p. 2

13 Hélène Bugat-Pujol, *Bleuette résiste, Son Trousseau de 1940 à 1949* (Paris: Jouve, 1998), p. 3

14 BillyBoy, "Bleuette: The Ideal Little Girl," *Doll News*, Winter, 1990, pp. 12-21

15 Couderc, op.cit. p. 19

16 *La Semaine de Suzette*, No. 42, October, 1927

17 Theimer, *Madame la Poupée Bleuette*, p. 8

Chapter 4

18 Porot et al., op.cit. p. 6

19 Bugat-Pujol, "Through '*Tante Jacqueline*,' p. 2

20 Ibid. p. 3

21 Colette Merlen, *Bleuette, Poupée de la Semaine de Suzette* (Paris: Les Editions de l'Amateur, 1992), p. 34

22 Bugat-Pujol, "A Bleuette Without Ambiguity," p. 4

23 Ibid.

24 Porot et al., op.cit. p. 163

25 Ibid.

26 Constance Eileen King, *The Collector's History of Dolls* (New York: St. Martin's Press, 1977), p. 376

27 Constance Eileen King, *Jumeau, Prince of Dollmakers* (Cumberland: Hobby House Press, 1983), p. 106

28 BillyBoy, *Bleuette: La Petite Fille Modèle de la collection BillyBoy* (Paris: Maeght Editions, 1993), p. 707

29 BillyBoy, "The Philosophy of Bleuette" (www.fondationtanagra.com, 1-01)

30 Ibid.

31 Hélène Bugat-Pujol, "Identity Crisis" (*L'univers de Suzette*, www.poupendol.com, 5-2001)

32 BillyBoy, "The Philosophy of Bleuette" (Fondation Tanagra, www.fondation tanagra.com)

33 BillyBoy, *Bleuette: La Petite Fille Modèle de la collection BillyBoy*, p. 336

Chapter 5

34 Anne-Marie Porot, *Bambino—Le Petit Frère de Bleuette* (Paris: Collection Connaissance Raisonee de la Poupee et du Jouet Anciens, 1999), p. 2

35 Porot et al., *S.F.B.J., Captivating Children*, p. 145

36 Porot, *Bambino*, p. 65

37 Andrew Tabbat, "Bécassine and Bleuette, Two Friends of Suzette," *Doll News*, Spring 2000, p. 54

38 Ibid.

PART II: THE WARDROBE

Chapter 6

[39] Sheryl Williams, "Editorial," *Doll Costuming*, January 2002, p. 78

[40] François Theimer, "Bleuette—Suzette's Week and Bambino," *Doll Reader*, May 1984, p. 99

[41] Theimer, *Madame La Poupée Bleuette*, p. 14

Chapter 7

[42] BillyBoy, *Bleuette: La Petite Fille Modèle de la collection BillyBoy*, pp.132-133

[43] Ibid. p. 280

[44] Bugat-Pujol, *Bleuette Résiste*, p. 1

[45] Ibid. p. 2

[46] Ibid. p. 1

[47] Ibid. p. 2

[48] Nicole Ward Jouve, "Gold Rush Rue Everlor," in Ian Breakwell and Paul Hammond, eds., *Seeing in the Dark: A Compendium of Cinema Going* (Serpents Tail, 1991)

PART III: REFERENCE

Appendix A

[49] Porot et al., op cit. p. 163

Appendix B

[50] Merlen, op.cit. p. 199

[51] H.C. Cradock, *Josephine and Her Dolls* (London: Blackie & Son, Ltd., 1918), p. 14

BIBLIOGRAPHY

A Suggested Reading List about Bleuette

Almquist-Bois, Gertrude & Suzanne Gautrot. *Nous Habillons Bleuette, 1905-1922*. Paris: Centre d'Études et de Recherches sur la Poupée, 1987.

Bazin, Albert. *Les Chapeaux de Bleuette*. Paris: chez l'auteur, 2000.

Breakwell, Ian & Paul Hammond, eds. *Seeing in the Dark: A Compendium of Cinema Going*. Serpents Tail, 1991.

BillyBoy. *Bleuette: La Petite Fille Modèle de la collection BillyBoy*. France: Maeght Editions, 1993.

_____. "Bleuette: The Ideal Little Girl." *Doll News*, Winter 1990, pp. 12-21.

_____. "The Philosophy of Bleuette." *fondationtanagra*. 1-2001. http://www.fondationtanagra.com.

BillyBoy Club. "A la Rencontre de Bleuette." *Bulletin, Des collectionneurs de la Poupée Bleuette*. June 1990.

Bristol, Olivia. *Les Poupées*, adaptation française de Julie Huline-Guinard. Paris: Librarie Gründ, 1997.

Buck, Anne. *Clothes and the Child*. New York: Holmes & Meier, 1996.

Bugat-Pujol, Hélène. "A Bleuette Without Ambiguity." *L'univers de Suzette*. 8-2001. http://www.poupendol.com.

_____. "Bleuette en Photos." *L'univers de Suzette*. 6-2001. http://www.poupendol.com.

_____."Identity Crisis." *L'univers de Suzette*. 5-2001. http://www.poupendol.com.

_____. "Portrait of Bleuette." *L'univers de Suzette*. 7-2001. http://www.poupendol.com.

_____. *Bleuette Résiste: Son Trousseau de 1940 à 1949*. Paris: Jouve, 1998.

_____. *Suzette, Gentille Cousette*. Paris: chez l'auteur, 1999.

_____. "Through 'Tante Jacqueline'." *L'univers de Suzette*. 12-2001. http://www.poupendol.com.

Buschbom, Marion. *Dressing Bleuette: A Collection of her Wardrobe Patterns*, translated/adapted by the author. U.S.A: 1999.

Catalogues de Bleuette. Paris: Editions Gautier-Languereau, 1916-1960.

Charles-Milius, Marie-Edith. *Nous Habillons Bleuette, 1922-1933*. Paris: Centre d'Études et de Recherches sur la Poupée, 1998.

Coleman, Dorothy S., Elizabeth A. & Evelyn J. *The Collector's Encyclopedia of Dolls, Vol. II*. New York: Crown Publishers, Inc., 1986.

_____. *The Collector's Encyclopedia of Dolls' Clothes, Costumes in Miniature: 1700-1929*. New York: Crown Publishers, Inc. 1975.

Couderc, Marie-Anne. *Bécassine inconnue*. Paris: CNRS Editions, 2000.

Cradock. H.C., *Josephine and Her Dolls*. London: Blackie & Son, Ltd., 1918.

Dunham, Mary E. *The One Stitch Dropped,* Philadelphia, PA: Columbia Book Co., 1899.

Formanek-Brunell, Miriam. *Made to Play House*, New Haven: Yale University Press, 1993.

Gautrot, Suzanne, "Flying Over This Universe." *L'univers de Suzette*. 5-2001. http://www.poupendol.com.

Gautrot, Suzanne & Samy Odin. *Bleuette: Haute Couture Pour Une Poupée*. Paris: Musée de la Poupée, Cercle Privé de la Poupée, 1994.

Goodfellow, Caroline G. *The Ultimate Doll Book*. New York: Dorling Kindersley, 1993.

King, Constance Eileen. *The Collector's History of Dolls*. New York: St. Martin's Press, 1977.

_____. *Jumeau, Prince of Dollmakers*. London: New Cavendish Books, 1983.

Kybalová, Ludmila, et al. *Pictorial Encyclopedia of Fashion*, trans. Claudia Rosoux. New York: Crown Publishers, Inc., 1968, 1972.

La Semaine de Suzette. Paris: Editions Gautier-Languereau, 1905-1940, 1946-1960.

Merlen, Collette. *Bleuette: Poupée de la Semaine de Suzette.* Paris: Les Editions de l'Amateur, 1992.

Odin, Samy. *Les Poupées de la S.F.B.J. 1899-1957.* Italy: Eurografica, 1999.

Odin, Samy, en collaboration avec le Cercle Privé de la Poupée. "Bleuette: Haute Couture pour une Petite Poupée." Paris: Cercle Privé de la Poupée, 1994.

Olian, JoAnne, ed. *Children's Fashions: 1860-1912.* New York: Dover Publications, 1994.

Pedagogical Survey. "The Educational Value of Dolls," December 1909, p. 9.

Porot, Anne-Marie. *Bambino—Le Petit Frère de Bleuettte.* Paris: Collection Connaissance Raisonée de la Poupée et du Jouet Anciens, 1999.

Porot, Anne-Marie et al. *S.F.B.J., Captivating Character Children.* Cumberland, Maryland: Hobby House Press, 1986.

Rait, Lila. "Bleuette in Australia," *Antique Doll Collector,* Vol. 2, No. 5 (1999), pp. 30-31.

Real, Susan. *"Bécassine Cherche Son Origine." Doll Reader,* Dec/Jan. 1983-1984, pp. 75-77.

Rose, Clare. *Children's Clothes.* New York: Holmes & Meiers, Drama Book Publishers, 1989.

Sirkis, Susan. *Wardrobe for a Little Girl, 1900-1910.* Wish Booklet Vol. X (1972) Reston, VA; published by the author.

Smith, Patricia. *French Dolls.* Paducah, Kentucky: Collector Books, 1979.

Sura, Agnes. "Bleuette and her Wardrobe, 1922." *Doll News,* Spring 1997, pp. 37-40.

_____. "But Who is this Doll, Bleuette?" *Antique Doll Collector,* Vol.2, No. 7 (1999), pp. 20-24.

Tabbat, Andrew. "Bécassine and Bleuette, Two Friends of Suzette." *Doll News,* Spring 2000, pp. 52-55.

_____. "Happy Birthday, Bécassine." *Doll Reader,* February 1996, pp. 74-77.

_____. "Louis Vuitton's Bécassine Dolls." *Doll News,* Winter 1995.

Terrie, Bernard. "Nanette...a doll to play with." *Gildebrief,* Vol. 3, No. 2 (1995), pp. 48-50.

The New Dressmaker, New York, Butterick Publishing Co., 1921.

Theimer, François. "Bleuette, Still on the Carpet, or Polichinelle Battles Windmills." *Polichinelle,* Vol. 6, p. 94-9, (1997), pp. 94-99.

_____. "Bleuette's Dress-up Costumes." *Polichinelle,* Vol. 2 (1993), pp. 108-199.

_____. "Bleuette, Suzette's Week and Bambino,". *Doll Reader,* May 1984, pp. 96-99.

_____. *La Poupée Modèle,* Vol. I, Paris: Editions Polichinelle, 1997.

_____. *La Poupée Modèle,* Vol. II, 1876-1885. Annapolis, Maryland: Gold Horse Publishing, 1998.

_____. *Madame la Poupée Bleuette.* Paris: Les Editions de l'Amateur, 1990.

_____. "Not Just Any Doll Can be Bleuette." *Polichinelle,* No. 27-30 (1993), pp. 5-21.

_____. "Not Just Any Doll Can be Bleuette." *A French Tapestry,* pp. 97-105. United Federation of Doll Clubs, 1998.

_____. "The Genuine Benjamine from *La Semaine de Suzette.*" *Polichinelle,* Vol. 6 (1997), pp. 94-97.

Verschoor, Olga. *Les Trousseaux du Temps Jadis.* Imprime en C.E.E.: *Hatier Littérature Générale,* 1996.

Welker, Lauren. "Introducing Bleuette's Pattern Wardrobe for 1927." *Doll Reader,* June/July 1986, pp. 224-225.

Welker, Lauren and Virginia Heyerdahl. *A 1927 Wardrobe for Suzette* (a reprinted, collected series of articles). Harrisburg, PA: *Doll Reader* magazine, 1998.

Williams, Sheryl. "Editorial," *Doll Costuming,* January 2002, p. 78.

Current Newsletters for Bleuette Collectors

Chères Amies de Bleuette Revue

Barbara C. Hilliker, Editor & Publisher

4515 Walking Stick Lane

Gainesville, GA 30506-5138

Bleuette's World

Agnes Sura, Editor

8 Trails End

Queensbury, NY 12804

SEWING RESOURCES

One of the challenges in sewing for Bleuette is finding appropriate fabrics and trims in the correct scale. In your local area, you should look for fabric stores that cater to quilters, as they usually carry an excellent stock of cotton fabrics. Or you may contact any of the following sources, which are known among doll costumers for being able to provide appropriate small-scale fabric and trims.

Genevieve Haberly
Genevieve's
832 Laurelhurst
Eugene, OR 97402

Louise Hedrick
LH Studio
1280 Orchard Lane
Elm Grove, WI 53122

Debbie Porchia
Mini-Magic
3910 Patricia Drive
Columbus, OH 43220

Janice Naibert
janicenaibert@erols.com

Cat's Paw
(manufacturers of fine doll jewelry, brass accessories, miniature trunks, and hardware)
336 Candlewood Lake Rd.
Brookfield, CT 06804
203-775-4717
catspawonline.com

G Street Fabrics
Mail Order Service
12240 Wilkins Ave.
Rockville, MD 20852

Keepsake Quilting
Route 25B
P.O. Box 1618
Centre Harbor, NH 03226-1618

In addition, there are many fabric resources on the internet. You may also find local area resources in fine sewing magazines and or at large needlework shows.

Photos by Jack Hilliker, except as noted below.

Robert M. Talbot, Talbot Studio
Pages: 6; 7; 12; 13; 15; 62, top; 69; 89, bottom right; 109; 121; 167; 169; Back cover, photos 1, 2 and 4

Theriault's Auctions
Pages: 11, 23

Walter Pfeiffer
Page 17

Joyce Coughlin
Pages: 19, top; 77; 99, bottom; 104, bottom

Patsy Moyer
Page 27

Monica Selby
Pages: 41; 87; 119; 164; Back cover, photo 3

Barbara Earnshaw-Cain
Page 42

Maree Studio
Pages: 44; 66, both top photos; 84–85; 89, top left and right; 105; 110, all photos; 111; 143; 149; 153; 157; 161

Atha Kahler
Pages: 51, top right; 95, bottom; 106, bottom right; 108; 116, top

Galeries de Chartres Auction
Pages: 53, top; 90, bottom; 91, bottom; 139

Doris Lechler
Pages: 53, right top and bottom; 129; 130, top

Mary Lou Ziller
Page 55, bottom right

Tomoko Fujii
Page 55, top

Ruth Brown
Pages: 65, bottom right; 92; 93, both photos; 94, left; 96, top; 102, top and bottom; 114, top; 117, top; 127, top; 136, bottom; 138, right

Courtesy UFDC
Page 80

Beatrice Dockter
Page 83

Marvyle Walker
Page 103, bottom

Deanna Pinizotto
Page 106, top

Daniel Bugat-Pujol
Pages: 115, top; 124, top

Becky Moncrief
Pages: 116, bottom; 135, bottom

The author would like to extend her deep appreciation to all who shared their dolls and their wardrobes for this book.

Louise Hedrick
Deanna Pinizotto
Hélène Bugat-Pujol
Suzanne Gautrot
Colette Bauer
Samy Odin
Guido Odin
Joyce Coughlin
Ruth Brown
Marvyle Walker
Marcene Oxford
Nadine Houy
Pat Randolph
Doris Lechler

Janice Thompson
Mary Lou Ziller
Marion Sullivan
Barbara Harter
Lynn Kublank
Jane Geroulis
Lucia Kirsch
Jean Theaker
Beatrice Dockter
Theodora Spaulding
Virginia Vinton
Georgia Henry
Sue Kinkade
Nancy Inglin

Tomoku Fujii
Mary K. Workman
Betty Fronefield
Atha Kahler
Ann M. Harris
Marian Allen
June Hays
Elsa McCallum
Janice Naibert
Evelyn Phillips
Karen Gloster
Carolyn Lindsay
Frances Powell
Mary Jane Brummer

Michele Thorpe
RoseAnn Wells
Ann Miles
Andrew Tabbat
Becky Moncrief
Chad Allman
Paddy Dignan
Sharon Geisen
Nancy Haneline
Laure Kagen
Sylvia Kleindinst
Jan Wallace
Patsy Moyer
Shirley Darmohray

Bradley Justice
Betty Moriarty
Sonya Shapiro

Galeries de Chartres
Auction
Owners: Jean-Pierre
Lelievre, Pascal
Maiche, Alain Paris
1 bis, pl. General-de-
Gaulle,
F-2800 Chartres, France
Phone: 011 2 37 84 04 33
FAX: 011 2 37 34 71

Theriault's Auctions
P.O. Box 151
Annapolis, MD 21404
Phone: 410-224-3655
FAX: 410-224-2515
www.theriaults.com

Special thanks go to
Scott Coughlin, who
created the beautiful
handmade altar shown
in the top photo
on page 19.

Additional Captions

Pages 6-7
Through the decades, Bleuette took on a variety of appearances. From left: the saucy-looking 301, shown in close-up, was the fourth doll to be made as Bleuette; the Première was, as her name proclaims, the first (see page 41 for more on this doll); the 6/0 was the second Bleuette (see page 47 for more); the SFBJ 60 8/0 was the third incarnation of Bleuette (see page 169 for more); and the 301 produced after World War II has an especially pale finish to her face (see page 167).

Pages 12-13
A gathering of Bleuettes includes, from left: a Première; a 6/0; an SFBJ 60 8/0 in a polished cotton romper; a 301 wearing a French-made dress of vintage fabric and a replaced human-hair wig; and another 301, garbed in an updated version of the "Casino" dress (see page 89).

Pages 84–85
The Première Bleuette is surrounded by her trousseau, stitched by her owner, Louise Hedrick, who researched each pattern and selected authentic fabrics and trims. Descriptions are from left to right, from front to rear. The year and number indicate the issue of *La Semaine de Suzette* in which the pattern appeared. The antique flat-topped trunk, covered in its original blue paper, has a lid lined with antique toys and china. Inside is a nightgown of antique batiste with scalloped cuffs and collar: *Chemise de nuit festonée*. #28, 1909. *Robe de Casino*, on the right, is new batiste and Swiss embroidery: #25-26, 1906. In front of the trunk is *Robe empire*, pink and green silk taffeta: #17, 1908. *Robe d'été*, is blue and ivory antique dimity cotton with a "transparency" of blue silk: #24, 1908. *Robe empire* is of brown and tan silk taffeta: #17, 1909. *Tablier de dimanche* is white-work pinafore, hand-embroidered on antique batiste: #13, 1909. *Robe de Casino* is made from an antique baby dress with hand-embroidered flounces: #25-26, 1906. *Robe de toile avec guimpe de mousseline* is rose silk taffeta; antique dimity is used for the blouse: #24, 1909. *Robe habillée avec guimpe* is a belted soutache dress of antique gold silk taffeta, antique soutache and ivory silk guimpe: #50-52, 1907. Another *Robe d'été* is antique aqua nainsook, with turquoise silk chain-stitching and satin ribbon: #20-21, 1907. *Chapeau* is turquoise straw, wired, with matching satin ribbons and plumes: #11, 1905. *Costume de quartier-maitre* is a mariner's sleeveless dress with jacket, and a beret in lined blue wool with antique cranberry silk soutache: #31-33, 1906. The Corset is ecru cotton satinette: #4, 1907. One more *Robe de Casino* is antique peach silk chiffon over silk taffeta: #25-26, 1906. The matching *capote-beguin* bonnet is from issue #47, 1907. This ensemble was made by Nadine Houy of Paris. A third *Robe d'été* is of peach and ivory dimity with antique satin ruching: #5, 1905. The *Chemise de jour brodée, pantalon fěrme, robe de dessous* is antique white-work with aqua silk embroidery: #49-51,1906. The *Tablier d'écolière* is olive and peach antique silk jacquard taffeta with peach silk feather-stitching: #45-46, 1906. The *Costume d'automobile* is antique red wool with burgundy silk top-stitching: #29-30, 1906.

Pages 164–165
From left: the head markings are clearly visible on this SFBJ 301; another Bleuette 301 has a well-preserved original paper stamp on its back; Maggie Salcedo illustrated many pages in the catalogs, including this one from the Winter 1930-31 Gautier-Languereau catalog; Bleuette's footwear was always marked with a B in an oval shape with pointed edges.

ABOUT THE AUTHOR

Barbara Hillker is widely acknowledged as one of the most knowledgeable English-speaking experts on Bleuette. Well-known to Bleuette lovers as the publisher and editor of the *Chère Amies de Bleuette Revue* newsletter since 1999, she began her research on the doll in the 1980s. In the course of this research, she has traveled extensively throughout the United States and France. She has written numerous articles on the subject, as well as presented programs and exhibitions about Bleuette nationally. A member of many doll collecting organizations, including the United Federation of Doll Clubs (UFDC), she has served in various capacities at UFDC national and regional conventions.

A patron member of the National Institute of American Doll Artists (NIADA), Mrs. Hilliker has edited several of the organization's souvenir journals. She is also a contributor to the book: *Dolls at 2000: A Celebration of Dolls at the Millennium*, edited by Rosalie Whyel.

Mrs. Hilliker has been a newspaper writer for *The Hoosier Times Magazine* (Crawfordsville, Indiana) and the *Daily Herald Telephone* (Bloomington, Indiana). The mother of five, grandmother of eleven and great-grandmother of one, she holds a degree in art history from California State University, Stanislaus.